I0819123

SUMAC BERRIES
ground fennel
Nonna's Blend
persian limes
thai chili
flakes
Paprika no oil
black
persian lime
WHITE
PEPPER
C.I.R. KESBEKE
AMSTERDAM
OREGANO
SINGLE ORIGIN SPICES BURLAP & BARREL
marash pepper
slow · small · simple
Bourbon Smoked Paprika
DILL
URFA
Dukkah
green peppercorns
curry powder
Bourbon Smoked Pepper
Cumin Seed
OREGANO
DRIED ROSEMARY
CAYENNE

Zariz

Zariz

100 Easy, Breezy, Tel Aviv–y Recipes

Adeena Sussman

AVERY
an imprint of Penguin Random House
New York

AVERY
an imprint of Penguin Random House LLC
1745 Broadway, New York, NY 10019
penguinrandomhouse.com

Book design by Ashley Tucker

Photography by Dan Perez; styling by Nurit Kariv

Library of Congress Cataloging-in-Publication Data

Names: Sussman, Adeena, author.
Title: Zariz : 100 easy, breezy, Tel Aviv-y recipes / Adeena Sussman.
Description: New York : Avery, an imprint of Penguin Random House, [2026] | Includes index.
Identifiers: LCCN 2025020567 (print) | LCCN 2025020568 (ebook) | ISBN 9780593719015 hardcover | ISBN 9780593719022 epub
Subjects: LCSH: Cooking, Israeli | Cooking—Israel—Tel Aviv | Jewish cooking | LCGFT: Cookbooks
Classification: LCC TX724 .S893 2026 (print) | LCC TX724 (ebook) | DDC 641.595694—dc23/eng/20250702
LC record available at https://lccn.loc.gov/2025020567
LC ebook record available at https://lccn.loc.gov/2025020568

Printed in China
10 9 8 7 6 5 4 3 2 1

The authorized representative in the EU for product safety and compliance is Penguin Random House Ireland, Morrison Chambers, 32 Nassau Street, Dublin D02 YH68, Ireland, https://eu-contact.penguin.ie.

For Dad (Stan) & Bette Sussman and Sharon & Ari Wieder.

This one's for you. Thanks for keeping me nourished in all the most important ways.

Contents

Introduction

When the going gets tough, the cooking gets easy.

That's been my mantra these past few years, which, admittedly, have been some of the hardest on record. Calm is increasingly elusive, instability has had a way of creeping into our lives no matter how much we may try to insulate ourselves, and the ups and downs show no sign of abating.

That's why I'm proposing your kitchen as even more of a refuge—as I know mine has become. A place where you make the rules, you set the tone, you choose the dress code (comfy pants, anyone?), and—most importantly—you get to decide what you cook and serve at your table every day.

Once you leave the house, all bets are off. But I'm here to reinforce the idea that at home, your kitchen island should be an island of calm.

In 2016 I moved to a country whose middle name might as well be Drama. In that time, through a pandemic, wars, marriage, and grandchildren (skipped the kids and went straight there, courtesy of my stepdaughter's family), I wrote eight cookbooks and hundreds of newsletters; filmed thousands of Instagram posts; and taught countless virtual and in-person cooking classes. In the process I became the luckiest person in the world, growing the most incredible community of passionate, smart, interested, and savvy cooks (that would be you; thank you so much! And if you're new, welcome).

תנובה
חלב

Without my realizing it, this very fast, full life was gradually nudging me toward a simpler, smoother way of cooking, one with a rhythm that relaxes, rather than taxes, both my brain and my body. One that relies on a slightly more edited—but no less versatile—group of staple ingredients and condiments culled mostly (but not exclusively) from Israeli, Middle Eastern, and Mediterranean traditions—with a healthy dose of American thrown in for good measure. My two previous cookbooks, *Sababa* and *Shabbat*, actually had a lot of quick, easy recipes—they just weren't defined that way. The stage was being set.

And so, this book: *Zariz*. Which, in Hebrew, means "quick" or "speedy."

So, what exactly does zariz mean to me? What it does not mean, most of the time, is three ingredients and five minutes—not that there's anything wrong with that! By all means do that whenever you want/need to. But I still believe in investing a bit of time and energy into the process. The sizzling of onions; the chopping of veggies; the searing, grilling, and stewing. The sounds, motions, and aromas of cooking that still, after all these years, make the kitchen my favorite place in the house. This can all feel easy, eminently doable, in the right surroundings—using streamlined recipes and instructions I've thought about an awful lot, so you don't have to.

Sometimes zariz means minimal pots and pans, or fewer cooking methods or pieces of equipment. Though there are a select few, you won't find a lot of recipes that use the stovetop, the oven, and an electric appliance all in the course of making one dish.

In other cases there might be a bit more prep on the front end, with the payoff on the back. Because to me, throwing everything in a pot or roasting pan, then lighting a flame or sending it to the oven for a few hours, unattended, is the ultimate cook's hall pass.

Most of the recipes in this book contain fewer than a "bat mitzvah," or a dozen ingredients—not including olive oil, salt, pepper, and lemons, which to me are such staples that I granted them to myself (and to you) as "free." Many of these recipes contain ten ingredients or less. Practically all of them fit on one page. I relished the challenge of delivering maximum flavor and creativity with minimal ingredients. Developing the recipes for this book caused me to take a long, hard look at every ingredient, technique, pot, or pan used and ask myself whether it deserved a place on the page. Everything had to have impact, which is why you'll see typically no more than one or two spices in a recipe—or a well-placed blend—in lieu of six different jars to open.

There are also more recipes in this book that are a complete meal-in-one: a starch and protein (and sometimes a veg) combined to make getting dinner on the table smoother than ever. That's not to say these aren't entertaining-worthy dishes—I have road tested them on many guests at dinner parties, Shabbat meals, and other hosting opportunities. And once people ask for the recipes, they're usually surprised at how short both the recipe's ingredient list and instructions are.

So take this book for a spin. Cook with it! Get those pages splattered, with folded-in edges and Post-its and notes in the margins. Make this book, and my recipes, your own.

Ultimately, my wish for you is to feel inspired, excited, and free to cook with ease, peace of mind, and delicious results. Thank you for taking this journey with me; I can't wait to meet you along the way.

PRESERVED LEMON
OCTOBER
19/01
קוטג'
תנובה

ALMOND MILK
BAHARAT
spice mix

Staples

Though you can buy most of the following products these days (and the spirit of this book as well as its author highly encourage you to do so), making them can be fun. A little time spent here will yield you months of use from this stable of staples. Make what you like, buy what you like—either way, having these in your pantry sets you up for success.

ALMOND MILK

MAKES 4 CUPS

A staple in my fridge, and the best plant-based milk you've ever tried. Omit the dates and vanilla for a neutral-flavored milk.

Cover 2 cups raw almonds with 2 inches cold water and soak in the refrigerator for 8 hours. (You can also cover with boiling water for 1 hour, leaving on the counter.) Drain and rinse well. Combine in a blender with 3¾ cups cold water, ¼ cup ice, and 2 large pitted Medjool dates (omit for unsweetened). Blend until smooth, 25 to 30 seconds. Pour carefully into a nut milk bag set over a large bowl. Squeeze to extract all liquid. (Use or freeze the solids for cookies or crackers.) Add 1 tablespoon vanilla extract or paste (omit for unsweetened) and ¼ teaspoon kosher salt. Store, tightly sealed, in the back of the refrigerator (not the door) for 3 to 4 days. Since the milk has no stabilizers or preservatives, it won't last much longer than that. Almond milk can be frozen, but leave room for expansion in its container. Defrost on the counter or in the fridge, then shake before using.

AMBA

MAKES 2 CUPS

My recipe for this Indian/Iraqi-Jewish condiment supplies the tangy funk of a 5-day pickle in less than 1 hour.

Peel 1 large or 2 medium completely unripe green-skinned mangoes (1 to 1¼ pounds total), such as Tommy Atkins variety; discard the peels. Grate the peeled mangoes on the large holes of a box grater straight into a medium saucepan. Add 2 cups water, 1 finely diced medium onion, 1½ tablespoons chopped jalapeño (with seeds), 2 tablespoons kosher salt, 3 chopped garlic cloves, 1 tablespoon ground turmeric, 1½ teaspoons yellow mustard seeds, 1 teaspoon ground fenugreek, ½ teaspoon ground cumin, and ½ teaspoon sweet paprika. Bring to a boil, reduce the heat to medium-low, and cook, stirring, until the mango and onion have softened and the liquid has reduced slightly, 20 to 25 minutes. Remove from the heat, cool slightly, then stir in 3 tablespoons freshly squeezed lemon juice and 1 teaspoon fish sauce (optional, but this gives a great funky tang). Transfer to a blender or food processor and puree until smooth and glossy, 20 seconds. Store in an airtight container in the refrigerator for 1 month.

BAHARAT SPICE BLEND

MAKES ¾ CUP

Great in savory dishes, but adding 1 teaspoon to the Chocolate-Cardamom Snacking Cake (page 236) or Pistachio Carrot Cake with Labaneh Frosting (page 230) lends something special.

In a bowl, combine 6 tablespoons ground cinnamon, 3 tablespoons finely ground black pepper, 2 tablespoons ground allspice, 2 teaspoons ground cardamom, 2 teaspoons freshly grated or ground nutmeg, 1 teaspoon ground ginger, and 1 teaspoon ground cloves. Store in an airtight container for up to 6 months.

ZA'ATAR SPICE BLEND

MAKES ¾ CUP

Za'atar can still be elusive on store shelves. Keep this easy homemade version on hand for an herby, tangy, sesame-studded boost.

Arrange 1 cup picked fresh hyssop (za'atar) leaves (or, more likely, oregano leaves) on a paper towel–lined microwave-safe plate and microwave, stopping and stirring every 30 seconds, until dry and crumbly, 2 to 2½ minutes. Crumble the dried leaves by hand or in a spice grinder until almost fine and combine them in a medium bowl with 3 tablespoons dried marjoram, 3 tablespoons toasted sesame seeds, 4 teaspoons dried thyme, 1 tablespoon ground sumac, and 1 teaspoon fine sea salt. Store in an airtight container for up to 3 months.

HARISSA

MAKES 1 GENEROUS CUP

Complex and nuanced in flavor, harissa is a welcome addition almost anywhere spice is requested. Make a double batch and freeze in tablespoon-sized cubes for up to 1 year.

Arrange 7 dried chiles de arbol and 1 dried guajillo chile (or 3 more chiles de arbol) in a bowl and cover with 1 cup boiling water; soak 1 hour. Drain, discard the water, then open the peppers and remove and discard as many seeds as you can; roughly chop the flesh. Toast 1 teaspoon each caraway, cumin, and coriander seeds in a small skillet over low heat until fragrant, 2 minutes. Cool, then grind them in a spice grinder to a fine powder. Add the spices to a food processor with 2 garlic cloves, the chopped chiles, ¼ cup olive oil, 1 tablespoon freshly squeezed lemon juice, 1 tablespoon sweet paprika, and 2 teaspoons kosher salt. Process the mixture and press it through a fine-mesh sieve into a bowl, discarding any solids. Pack the harissa into a jar with a tight-fitting lid, cover with another tablespoon of olive oil, and store in the fridge for up to 1 month, or freeze in airtight containers for up to 6 months.

HAWAIIJ SPICE BLEND

MAKES ¾ CUP

This mildly spicy Yemenite seasoning blend turns anything it touches—from soups to salad dressings—into gold.

Combine ¼ cup each finely ground black pepper and ground cumin, 3 tablespoons ground turmeric, and 2 tablespoons each ground cardamom and ground coriander in a bowl. If you're feeling ambitious, toast over very low heat in a skillet until fragrant, 1 to 2 minutes; transfer immediately to a plate to prevent the spices from burning. Transfer to an airtight jar or container for up to 6 months.

LABANEH

MAKES 2 CUPS

Fresh, creamy, and indispensable. Adding lemon juice lends extra fluff and flavor. The longer you strain, the thicker the end result.

Line a medium bowl with a large, clean kitchen towel. In another bowl, whisk together 4 cups whole-milk yogurt, 1 tablespoon freshly squeezed lemon juice, and 2 teaspoons kosher salt. Transfer to the towel-lined bowl. Gather two opposite sides of the towel and tie them into a knot, then loop the two remaining opposite sides through and tie them into a knot, leaving the ends for hanging. Find a space over a kitchen or bathroom sink or shower or tub (or large bowl). Hang the labaneh, letting the liquid drip. Drain a minimum of 4 hours (for a consistency similar to Greek yogurt) and a maximum of 24 (for something more like cream cheese). Transfer to an airtight container; refrigerate 1 month.

POMEGRANATE MOLASSES

MAKES 1 CUP

The perfect sweet-tangy combination makes it a favorite in dressings and glazes—or for drizzling.

In a small saucepan, whisk 5 cups pure pomegranate juice (fresh or bottled, such as Pom Wonderful brand) and 2 tablespoons honey. Bring to a low boil over medium-high heat; boil until reduced to 2 cups (use a measuring cup to gauge the volume), 25 minutes. Reduce the heat to medium-low. Simmer, stirring occasionally, until small bubbles form over the top. Reduce heat to low; simmer until the liquid is visibly thickened but not as thick as honey (it will thicken as it cools); bubbles will be foamy and small. Remove from the heat and dip a spoon into the molasses; if you run your finger over the back of the spoon, a distinct stripe will form. Refrigerate in an airtight container for up to 6 months.

TAHINI SAUCE

MAKES 2½ CUPS

A quick whisk yields an ethereally creamy, nutty dip/sauce/condiment that (confession time) I prefer to hummus.

In a large bowl, combine 1 cup pure tahini paste, 2 minced garlic cloves, and 2 teaspoons kosher salt. Whisk in ⅓ cup freshly squeezed lemon juice until incorporated, then whisk in ½ cup cold water until thick, creamy, and just pourable, 25 to 30 seconds. Thin with water or lemon juice and season with salt as needed. Refrigerate in an airtight container up to 4 days; let come to room temperature. Loosen with water and lemon juice to taste.

PRESERVED LEMONS

MAKES 2 CUPS

Almost as ubiquitous as fresh lemons in my kitchen. Time and sun do most of the work. An extra jar makes the perfect gift for a lucky friend; blend with a bit of olive oil for preserved lemon paste.

Wash a 24-ounce jar and its lid (preferably plastic) in soapy water; dry. Working with 8 lemons and 1 cup kosher salt, use a sharp knife to cut an X shape through each lemon so it is quartered but not cut all the way through. Working over a bowl, hold a lemon open in your hand. Pack a heaping tablespoon of the salt inside, close the lemon, and fit it into the jar. Repeat with the remaining lemons and salt, fitting the lemons in the jar as tightly as possible. Sprinkle more salt on the lemons as you go along. Juice will gush out of the lemons and fill the jar. If needed, add more freshly squeezed lemon juice to cover the salted lemons and fill the jar. Seal tightly, place the jar on a plate to catch any leaks, and leave it in a sunny place for at least 2 weeks and up to 3 months, flipping the jar occasionally and adding lemon juice during the first few days to keep the lemons covered with liquid. Refrigerate for up to 1 year.

SCHUG

MAKES 2 CUPS

If Beyoncé lived where I live, this would be the hot sauce in her bag. The combo of garlic, herbs, spices, and hot peppers is super versatile.

In a food processor, process 2 cups each packed fresh parsley and cilantro (including tender stems), 20 garlic cloves, 10 medium jalapeños (stemmed, seeds and veins intact), 2 teaspoons kosher salt, 2 teaspoons fresh lemon juice, and ½ teaspoon each ground cumin and freshly ground black pepper until smooth, adding 1 to 2 tablespoons water and scraping down the sides if needed, 1 minute. Transfer to an airtight container, cover with 2 tablespoons olive oil, seal, and refrigerate up to 1 month. (The schug will fade in potency and color but is totally usable.) You can freeze it in 1- or 2-tablespoon portions in ice cube trays or silicone freezer cubes, then pop into a Ziploc bag. Freeze up to 6 months.

GARLIC CONFIT

MAKES 1 CUP EACH ROASTED GARLIC CLOVES AND ROASTED GARLIC OIL (RECIPE CAN BE HALVED OR DOUBLED)

Spread on chicken; serve alongside pita instead of butter; add to soups and stews.

Preheat the oven to 250°F. Combine 1½ cups (35 to 40) peeled garlic cloves with 1 fresh thyme sprig and 1¼ cups olive oil in a small ceramic or metal ovenproof dish. Cover tightly with foil and bake until lightly golden and totally soft but not caramelized, 50 to 55 minutes. Refrigerate in an airtight container for up to 1 week.

Kitchen Notes

Cherry Tomatoes

1 pound = 3 cups

Feta

1 ounce = ¼ cup crumbled
4 ounces = 1 cup crumbled

Flour

Every baker weighs their flour differently; my standard cup of flour weighs 130 grams. I use the "scoop and level" method to measure; spoon or scoop flour out of a large container or bag into a measuring cup, sprinkling it in rather than packing it down. Continue until the measuring cup is just overfilled, then use a knife to level the flour to the top of the measuring cup, scraping excess flour back into the container.

Garlic

One head of garlic contains about 12 or 13 large cloves. One cup of garlic equals 35 to 40 whole cloves. Three minced garlic cloves equal 1 tablespoon.

Parmigiano Reggiano Cheese

I use a Microplane grater to freshly grate my parm. One ounce of cheese equals about 1½ cups measured in a dry measuring cup.

Lemon Juice and Zest

For our purposes, a standard lemon equals 3 tablespoons (or a drop more) lemon juice and a lightly packed 1 tablespoon finely grated zest (grated on a Microplane grater).

Kosher Salt

My standard is Diamond Crystal kosher salt. I prefer it for its even, balanced, not-too-salty salinity. If you are using Morton kosher salt or fine sea salt, use about half the amount.

Produce Weights

I added weights of fruits and vegetables where I felt it was essential to the recipe, but not everywhere.

Pot Sizes

In my kitchen. a small pot or saucepan is 1 to 2½ quarts; a medium is 2½ to about 4½ quarts; and a large is basically anything above 5 quarts.

Spatchcocking

To spatchcock a chicken, arrange a whole chicken breast side down on a cutting board. Use kitchen shears to cut out the backbone, then flip the chicken over and press down on the breast to flatten.

SHOPPING

Amba

The quality of amba imported from Israel to the United States remains a tad spotty; Galil brand is the most reliable of those. Teta brand amba, new to the market in the last few years, is made in the USA and available online. To make your own, see the recipe on page 14.

Harissa

New York Shuk, a boutique company based in Brooklyn, makes a delicious version. Pereg brand harissa contains more oil, has a vibrant red color, and is available in kosher stores and online. To make your own, see the recipe on page 15.

Labaneh

Karoun, the most widely available brand, is a good choice; thin with a little water if needed. To make your own, see the recipe on page 16.

Olive Oil

I live in a place with amazing local olive oil available year-round. If you don't, Bertolli Extra Virgin Olive Oil, available in supermarkets, is a great choice. My favorite brands of Israeli oil are La Boîte Moshe Oil, Ptora, Rish Lakish, and Sindyanna. La Boîte and Ptora can be found on Laboite.com, Rish Lakish at Onkaiten.com, and Sindyanna—an Arab-Jewish cooperative—on Kalustyans.com.

Schug

Trader Joe's makes a very good schug (they call it "Zhoug") for a reasonable price. It's not kosher certified, but all the ingredients are vegan. To make your own, see the recipe on page 17.

Silan (Date Syrup)

Date Lady and D'vash both make delicious date syrups and can be found both in stores and online.

Spices

Burlap & Barrel, New York Shuk, La Boîte, and Pereg are my most-frequented spice purveyors. They carry most of the Middle Eastern/Israeli spices needed for my recipes.

Tahini

So many excellent tahinis are now available in the United States and beyond. My favorites include Al Arz, Har Bracha, Soom Foods, and Seed + Mill, all easily found online. Whole Foods' 365 brand is a good-value buy.

Breakfast

Puff Pastry "Malawach" w/ the Works

Sunny Sheet Pan Shakshuka

Maple Tahini Oatmeal

Smoothie Quartet

- *Blueberry Halvah Smoothie*
- *Smoothie Yarok (Green Smoothie)*
- *Gingery Mango Labaneh Lassi*
- *Raspberry Almond Smoothie*

Family-Sized Potato & Cheese Boureka

Lemon-Cardamom Blueberry Muffins

Chewy Nut, Date & Chocolate Chip Energy Bars

Mediterranean Breakfast Scramble

Puff Pastry "Malawach" w/ the Works

SERVES 4 • ACTIVE TIME: 25 MINUTES • **TOTAL TIME:** 25 MINUTES

"Salad for breakfast" could be the tagline of life in Israel; a classic morning repast often includes vegetables chopped, shredded, or otherwise cut—but always raw. They're often served with something starchy, but I've hesitated to put malawach recipes in my previous books because the fried Yemenite pan-bread is typically sold frozen in kosher markets, making it hard to find (preparing it from scratch is complicated, too). But once I realized it's quite similar to puff pastry, I went to work using a standard frozen sheet to approximate the flaky layers of a malawach. Think salad, schug, eggs—everything you need to start the day off right.

½ cup pure tahini paste

6 tablespoons ice water

6 tablespoons freshly squeezed lemon juice (from 2 lemons)

1¼ teaspoons kosher salt, plus more for seasoning

1 garlic clove, minced

1 standard (9¾ × 10½-inch) frozen puff pastry sheet (such as Pepperidge Farm), thawed

4 or 5 Persian cucumbers, diced

3 medium vine-ripened tomatoes, diced

5½ tablespoons olive oil

Freshly ground black pepper

4 large eggs

Schug (page 17 or store-bought), for serving

1. Line a cutting board and a plate with parchment paper. In a medium bowl, whisk the tahini, ice water, 3 tablespoons of the lemon juice, 1 teaspoon of the salt, and the garlic until fluffy and creamy, 30 seconds. Arrange the pastry sheet on the cutting board. Use an inverted 4-inch bowl (or cookie cutter) and a paring knife to cut four 4-inch circles from the pastry;* remove and reserve the excess dough for another use. Arrange the circles on the plate and refrigerate for 5 minutes to firm up slightly.

2. Combine the cucumbers and tomatoes in a bowl and toss with the remaining 3 tablespoons lemon juice, 3 tablespoons of the olive oil, the remaining ¼ teaspoon salt, and pepper to taste. Heat a large (10- or 12-inch) lidded heavy skillet over medium heat. (You may be able to do these all at once, or in two batches.) Brush with ½ tablespoon of the olive oil, add the circles to the skillet, and cook, partially covered, until puffed, golden, and crisp, 3 to 4 minutes per side. Transfer to a plate.

3. Raise the heat to medium-high, add the remaining 2 tablespoons olive oil to the skillet, then crack all 4 eggs into the skillet and cook, spooning a little hot oil over the egg whites, until the whites are opaque and the edges are lacy, 3 to 4 minutes. Season with salt and pepper. Arrange a pastry round on a plate and top with some of the salad and a drizzle of the tahini. Top with an egg and serve with schug. (Serve extra salad and tahini on the side.)

**To make a family-sized malawach, arrange a 9-inch plate face down over the pastry and use a paring knife to cut a 9-inch circle from the pastry. (Or use a frozen malawach from your local kosher or Middle Eastern grocery store.)*

Sunny Sheet Pan Shakshuka

SERVES 4 • ACTIVE TIME: 25 MINUTES **• TOTAL TIME:** 50 MINUTES

2 large sweet potatoes (1¼ pounds), peeled and cut into ¾-inch cubes

2½ cups (12 ounces) orange or yellow cherry tomatoes

1 large orange or yellow bell pepper, sliced

1 large onion, sliced

7 tablespoons olive oil

2 teaspoons kosher salt, plus more for seasoning

1½ teaspoons ground cumin

½ teaspoon ground turmeric

½ teaspoon cayenne

One 7- to 8-ounce block feta cheese, patted dry

4 large eggs

½ large lemon

Freshly ground black pepper

I've made shakshuka—a typically spicy, saucy breakfast dish of Tunisian/Moroccan origin—every which way. Green, red, and white versions have appeared in my previous books, but never one in happy tones of yellow and orange—and never on a sheet pan. Enter this skilletless interpretation, which deconstructs the classic elements (tomatoes, peppers), adds sweet potatoes, and uses the oven to cook everything—including the eggs. The feta becomes slightly caramelized and golden, perfect for dividing among plates with the other elements.

1. Preheat the oven to 425°F. Arrange the sweet potatoes, tomatoes, bell peppers, and onions on a large rimmed baking sheet. In a small bowl, whisk together the olive oil, salt, cumin, turmeric, and cayenne. Drizzle ¼ cup of the seasoned oil over the vegetables and stir to coat. Nestle the block of feta in the center of the pan and drizzle the feta with an additional tablespoon of the oil mixture. Bake until the vegetables are soft and lightly browned around the edges and the feta is golden, 20 to 25 minutes.

2. Remove the baking sheet from the oven. Use a silicone spatula or wooden spoon to form four 4-inch wells at each corner of the baking sheet, leaving a 2-inch border of vegetables around each well. Add ½ tablespoon of the oil mixture to each well. Crack an egg into each well. Return the pan to the oven and bake until the egg whites are opaque and yolks are slightly runny, 4 to 5 minutes. Zest the lemon across the baking sheet, then squeeze the juice all over the veggies. Season with salt and pepper. Divide among four plates.

Maple Tahini Oatmeal

SERVES 2 • ACTIVE TIME: 10 MINUTES • **TOTAL TIME:** 10 MINUTES

With all due respect to overnight oats, I prefer my oatmeal hot. Simple and sweet-savory, this dish can be assembled in minutes but feels like an "investment breakfast." It's like the Quaker packet, only infused with the no-brainer, nutty surprise of tahini. Though the recipe calls for instant oats—which cut the cooking time by a third—if you don't mind more stirring, use steel-cut oats if you like.

- ⅔ cup instant oats*
- 2 cups oat or other milk, plus more as needed
- ½ teaspoon kosher salt
- ¼ teaspoon ground cinnamon, or more to taste
- 3 tablespoons maple syrup
- 1½ tablespoons pure tahini paste, plus more for drizzling
- 1 teaspoon pure vanilla extract

Toppings

- Sliced bananas
- Fresh berries
- Goji berries, dried cherries, or other dried fruit
- Toasted dried coconut
- Chopped toasted almonds
- Cacao nibs
- Pomegranate seeds

Combine the oats, milk, salt, and cinnamon in a medium saucepan. Bring to a low boil over medium heat and cook, stirring often, until the mixture has thickened and the oats are soft (add more milk if you like a thinner oatmeal), 1 to 2 minutes. Stir in the maple syrup, tahini, and vanilla. Divide between bowls and garnish with the toppings of your choice. Drizzle with more tahini, if desired.

**If you prefer to use steel-cut oats, the instructions are the same—just cook for 20 to 25 minutes.*

Smoothie Quartet

Smoothies! They're not just for breakfast. But I can think of no better way to start the day than with one of these blender drinks. Each one is colorful, packed with flavor, and inspired by the superior juice stands you'll find all over Tel Aviv (my favorite has been owned and operated by Tikvah Yitzchak [see photo, page 244] in the Carmel Market for decades). Whether it's the halvah in the blueberry smoothie, the mint in the Smoothie Yarok (green smoothie), the cardamom in the lassi, or the pomegranate juice in the Raspberry Almond Smoothie, they all have a twist that elevates the finished product. A regular blender works great, and a bullet-style blender produces extra-creamy, smooth results.

Blueberry Halvah Smoothie

MAKES 2½ CUPS • ACTIVE TIME: 5 MINUTES
TOTAL TIME: 6 MINUTES

1 cup frozen blueberries

¼ cup crumbled halvah*

1 cup milk of your choice

¼ cup ice

1 tablespoon whole or ground flaxseed

Pinch of ground cloves (optional)

Finely grated zest of 1 lemon, plus lemon wheels for garnish

1 teaspoon pure vanilla extract

Pinch of kosher salt

Combine all the ingredients in a blender and blend on high speed until smooth, 15 to 20 seconds. Pour into glasses and garnish with lemon wheels.

**Halvah can be replaced with 3 tablespoons pure tahini paste and 1 tablespoon sugar or honey.*

Raspberry Almond Smoothie

MAKES 2 CUPS • ACTIVE TIME: 3 MINUTES
TOTAL TIME: 5 MINUTES

¾ cup almond or other milk

½ cup ice

⅓ cup pomegranate juice

2 tablespoons almond butter

2 tablespoons honey or silan (date syrup), plus more to taste

1 cup frozen raspberries

Combine all the ingredients in a blender and blend on high speed until smooth, 15 to 20 seconds. If desired, add more honey to taste and reblend.

Smoothie Yarok (Green Smoothie)

MAKES 2 CUPS • ACTIVE TIME: 5 MINUTES
TOTAL TIME: 5 MINUTES

½ cup milk of your choice

½ cup lightly packed spinach leaves

½ cup diced fresh, frozen, or canned pineapple (drained if canned)

½ cup diced kiwi

5 or 6 fresh mint leaves, plus more for garnish

½ cup ice

2 tablespoons honey, plus more to taste

1 teaspoon pure vanilla extract

Pinch of kosher salt

Combine all the ingredients in a blender and blend on high speed until smooth, 15 to 20 seconds. If desired, add more honey to taste. Pour into glasses and garnish with mint leaves.

Gingery Mango Labaneh Lassi

MAKES 2½ CUPS • ACTIVE TIME: 5 MINUTES
TOTAL TIME: 6 MINUTES

1¼ cups cubed fresh (or 1½ cups frozen) mango

¾ cup labaneh or Greek yogurt

2 tablespoons freshly squeezed lime juice, plus more to taste

2 tablespoons honey, plus more to taste

1-inch piece fresh ginger, peeled, plus more to taste

⅛ teaspoon ground cardamom, plus more to taste

¼ cup ice, or more if desired

Pinch of ground turmeric

Pinch of kosher salt

Combine all the ingredients in a blender and blend on high speed until smooth, 15 to 20 seconds. If desired, add more lime juice, honey, ginger, and cardamom to taste and reblend.

pyrex

Gingery Mango
Labaneh Lassi
Raspberry Almond
Smoothie
Blueberry Halvah
Smoothie
Smoothie Yarok
(Green Smoothie)

Family-Sized Potato & Cheese Boureka

SERVES 4 AS A MAIN COURSE, 8 AS A SNACK
ACTIVE TIME: 15 MINUTES • **TOTAL TIME:** 60 MINUTES

Frozen puff pastry and I had a long separation, but lately we've reconciled and are back in each other's good graces. Few convenience products provide so much rich luxury for something you'd probably never make at home. If you can find a butter-based French one, by all means press it into service here. But the standard, dairy-free supermarket version works well, too. Two sharp cheeses and grainy mustard add punch to the mashed potato filling. Serve with briny pickles and spicy condiments for an extra kick.

1 medium-large potato (1 pound), peeled and cut into 1-inch chunks

¾ cup (3 ounces) grated sharp Cheddar cheese

¾ cup (3 ounces) crumbled feta cheese

¼ cup thinly sliced scallion greens

2 tablespoons olive oil

2 tablespoons grainy Dijon mustard

1 teaspoon kosher salt

¼ teaspoon freshly ground black pepper

1 large egg, beaten, plus another beaten egg for brushing

2 standard frozen puff pastry sheets (such as Pepperidge Farm), thawed

2 tablespoons sesame seeds

Flaky sea salt, for sprinkling

Pickles, Schug (page 17 or store-bought), and/or Harissa (page 15 or store-bought), for serving

1. Place the potatoes in a medium pot and cover with 2 inches of water. Bring to a boil, reduce the heat, cover, and simmer until the potatoes are tender, 15 minutes. Drain and cool to room temperature, about 15 minutes,* then transfer to a large bowl and mash until smooth (you should have about 1¼ cups mashed). Add the cheddar, feta, scallions, olive oil, mustard, salt, pepper, and egg and stir until well incorporated.

2. Arrange two racks in the top and bottom thirds of the oven; preheat to 425°F.

3. Arrange each piece of puff pastry on a piece of parchment paper and roll it out slightly to about 11 × 11 inches (if it gets soft, pop it into the freezer for a few minutes). Transfer each piece on its parchment to a large baking sheet. Arrange half the filling in a triangular shape over half of each piece, leaving a 1-inch border around the edges.

4. Brush the inside border of each pastry with the second beaten egg, then use the parchment to fold the other half of the pastry over the filling. Seal and crimp each triangle with a fork, brush with egg, sprinkle each with half the sesame seeds, and then sprinkle with flaky salt. Bake until deeply golden and puffed, switching the sheets midway through, 23 to 24 minutes total. Cool for 5 minutes, then use a large knife to cut each into four (or eight) equal-sized triangles.

**To cool potatoes quickly, spread them out on a baking sheet in an even layer.*

Lemon-Cardamom Blueberry Muffins

MAKES 12 MUFFINS
ACTIVE TIME: 25 MINUTES • **TOTAL TIME:** 45 MINUTES

Blueberry muffins . . . so simple, and so simple to mess up. Using oil instead of butter keeps them tender and moist, as does making sure to avoid overmixing the batter and overbaking. Zingy lemon zest and earthy, floral cardamom make these perfect for pairing with either coffee or herbal tea. If you're serving these the next day, warm them, then split and serve with a generous pat of salted butter.

- 1¼ cups (250 grams) sugar
- Finely grated zest of 1 large lemon
- 1½ teaspoons ground cardamom
- 2¼ cups (293 grams) all-purpose flour
- 1 tablespoon (15 grams) baking powder
- ½ teaspoon (3 grams) kosher salt
- ⅔ cup (165 grams/ml) whole milk
- ½ cup (110 grams/ml) neutral oil
- 1 large egg
- 2 teaspoons (10 grams/ml) pure vanilla extract or paste
- 1½ cups (9 ounces/ 255 grams) fresh or frozen (unthawed) blueberries
- Softened salted butter, for serving (optional)

1. Preheat the oven to 400°F. Line each compartment of a standard 12-cup muffin tin with a double layer of paper liners.

2. In a large bowl, combine the sugar, lemon zest, and cardamon; rub with your fingertips until fragrant, 15 seconds. Whisk in the flour, baking powder, and salt. In another medium bowl, whisk together the milk, oil, egg, and vanilla until smooth. Very gently fold the wet ingredients into the dry ingredients until incorporated (the batter texture will resemble thick hummus). Gently fold in the blueberries. Divide the batter among the liners (it should come up to just under the top). Bake until golden and domed and the centers feel tender-firm when pressed, 18 to 19 minutes. Transfer to a wire rack to cool. Serve warm or at room temperature with butter, if desired.

Chewy Nut, Date & Chocolate Chip Energy Bars

MAKES 12 BARS • ACTIVE TIME: 10 MINUTES **• TOTAL TIME:** 30 MINUTES

I am of the theory that anything a store-bought energy bar can do, a homemade one can do better. For starters, taste: With very few ingredients, these nutty, chewy, and very satisfying treats pack a nutrition punch of fiber and protein thanks to tahini, almonds, coconut, and dates. Fudgy Medjool dates are important here, as they lend moisture, stickiness, and the perfect sweetness the recipe requires.

- 1½ cups (170 grams) rolled oats
- 1 cup (140 grams) raw almonds
- ⅓ cup (30 grams) unsweetened shredded coconut
- ¼ cup (35 grams) sesame seeds
- 1 pound (460 grams) Medjool dates (20 or 21 large, or 16 jumbo)
- 1 teaspoon (5 grams/ml) pure vanilla extract
- ¼ cup (65 grams/60 ml) pure tahini paste
- ¾ teaspoon (2 grams) flaky sea salt
- ¾ cup (4½ ounces/130 grams) semisweet or bittersweet chocolate chips

1. Preheat the oven to 350°F. Line both a rimmed baking sheet and a 9-inch square or 8 × 10-inch rectangular baking pan with parchment paper.

2. Place the oats, almonds, coconut, and sesame seeds on the prepared baking sheet and roast, stirring once midway through, until the oats, coconut, and sesame seeds are toasted and the almonds are fragrant, 10 to 11 minutes. Remove from the oven and cool completely. Meanwhile, pit the dates and measure them; you should have about 1⅓ cups packed, pitted dates. If you don't, add one or two more. Add the dates to a food processor with the vanilla, tahini, oats, almonds, coconut, sesame seeds, and ½ teaspoon of the flaky salt.

3. Process until everything is chopped fine and the mixture holds together and is slightly sticky when pinched, 25 to 30 seconds. Add the chocolate chips and pulse five times. Press firmly into the prepared pan, top with the remaining ¼ teaspoon flaky salt, and chill for 10 minutes. Remove from the fridge and cut into 12 squares or rectangles. Wrap individually in wax paper or parchment, if desired. Bars will last wrapped on the counter for 5 days, or refrigerated in an airtight container for up to 2 weeks.

Mediterranean Breakfast Scramble

SERVES 4 • ACTIVE TIME: 15 MINUTES **• TOTAL TIME:** 25 MINUTES

You could spend all your time perfecting your French omelet skills, or you could make scrambled eggs, which are infinitely more forgiving and adaptable. Here, salty, cheesy, herby, and creamy ingredients combine to create the greatest breakfast mishmash. Cottage cheese adds protein and makes the eggs extra luscious; a feta swap-in is a worthy substitute, so you can't go wrong no matter what you opt for. Herbs, olives, and cheeses are interchangeable, making this the ultimate mix-and-match experience.

- 8 large eggs
- ⅔ cup full-fat cottage cheese (or ½ cup/2 ounces crumbled feta)
- 3 tablespoons olive oil
- 1 medium zucchini, cut into ¼-inch dice
- 4 scallions, thinly sliced
- 1 tablespoon finely diced jalapeño
- ½ teaspoon kosher salt, plus more to taste
- 4 oil-packed sun-dried tomatoes, drained and chopped (or ½ cup cherry tomatoes, quartered)
- 2 tablespoons sliced pitted olives of your choice
- ½ cup (¾ ounce) finely grated Parmigiano Reggiano cheese
- ¼ cup finely chopped dill, plus more for garnish
- Toast or crusty bread, for serving

In a large bowl, whisk the eggs, then stir in the cottage cheese to combine. Heat the olive oil in a large (at least 10-inch) nonstick skillet over medium-high heat until it shimmers. Add the zucchini and cook, resisting the urge to stir, until the underside is golden, 4 to 5 minutes. Add the scallions, jalapeño, and ¼ teaspoon of the salt and cook, stirring, until softened, 2 minutes. Reduce the heat to medium-low and stir in the egg and cheese mixture along with the tomatoes and olives and cook, stirring constantly, until the eggs are creamy but still slightly runny, 4 to 5 minutes. Stir in the parm, dill, and remaining ¼ teaspoon salt (if using feta, add only a pinch of salt). Season with additional salt to taste. Divide among four plates, garnish with the dill, and serve with toast.

Dips, Spreads & Condiments

Super Seeded Crackers

MAKES 15 APPROXIMATELY 2-INCH CRACKERS
ACTIVE TIME: 10 MINUTES • **TOTAL TIME:** 40 MINUTES

You'll want to keep these gluten-free seeded wonders on hand for cheese plates, soups, salads, dips, and snacking. The dried onion flakes are something I've been eating since I was a kid, when my mom would crisp them in the pan to add to our omelets. Here they add an irresistible toastiness in combination with virtually every other seed you can think of. No flour here: Flax and tahini hold the crackers together like magic.

- ½ cup raw sunflower seeds
- ½ cup raw pepitas (pumpkin seeds)
- ⅓ cup white sesame seeds
- ¼ cup ground flaxseed
- ¼ cup fine almond meal
- ¼ cup dried onion flakes
- 3 tablespoons poppy seeds
- 1 tablespoon nigella or black sesame seeds (or more white sesame seeds)
- ½ teaspoon kosher salt
- ½ teaspoon dried red pepper flakes
- ½ cup boiling water
- 3 tablespoons pure tahini paste

Preheat the oven to 350°F. In a medium heatproof bowl, combine the sunflower seeds, pepitas, sesame seeds, flaxseed, almond meal, onion flakes, poppy seeds, nigella seeds, salt, and red pepper flakes. Add the boiling water, stir to incorporate, and let sit until the mixture has absorbed the water and holds together, 10 minutes. Stir in the tahini until incorporated. Gather the mixture into a 5-inch disc and place it in the center of a large piece of parchment paper. Cover with another piece of parchment and roll out to ⅛-inch thickness (roughly 12 × 14 inches in size). Transfer to a baking sheet, peel off and discard (or reuse) the top layer of parchment, and bake until the edges are crisp and darkened and the center is dry, 19 to 22 minutes. Cool completely and break into pieces. Crackers can be stored in an airtight container for up to 5 days, or frozen for up to 3 months, then thawed before using.

Smoky Tomato & White Bean Dip

MAKES 2 CUPS • ACTIVE TIME: 5 MINUTES **• TOTAL TIME:** 40 MINUTES

Dips shouldn't cause a dip in your energy level, meaning simplicity is key. Here, all the main elements roast together on one sheet pan, a method that removes excess moisture, concentrates flavor, and helps the mixture absorb the mild spice and smokiness from the paprika and harissa that get added while the beans and tomatoes are still warm. Sage is the surprise element; it adds deep, dusky herbiness that enhances the proceedings. This is great with veggies or pita chips, and also works as a divine sandwich spread.

- 3 cups (1 pound) cherry tomatoes
- One 15-ounce can cannellini beans, drained and rinsed
- 10 garlic cloves
- 6 large sage leaves, thinly sliced
- ⅓ cup olive oil, plus more for drizzling
- 1½ teaspoons kosher salt, plus more for seasoning
- ½ teaspoon smoked paprika
- 2 teaspoons Harissa (page 15 or store-bought), or more to taste
- Red Pita Chips (recipe follows), for serving

Preheat the oven to 350°F. Scatter the tomatoes, beans, garlic, and sage on a large rimmed baking sheet, drizzle with the olive oil and 1 teaspoon of the salt, and toss to coat. Roast, stirring once midway through, until the tomatoes begin to burst and have released some of their juices and the garlic is soft and golden, 30 to 35 minutes. Cool, reserving 3 or 4 garlic cloves and 2 tablespoons of the tomatoes for topping. Transfer the rest to a bowl. Add the smoked paprika, harissa, and remaining ½ teaspoon salt and mash with a potato masher (or process with an immersion blender) until chunky-smooth. Season with more salt to taste, top with the reserved garlic and tomatoes, and drizzle with olive oil. Serve with red pita chips. Dip can be refrigerated in an airtight container for up to 4 days.

Red Pita Chips

SERVES 8 • ACTIVE TIME: 5 MINUTES **• TOTAL TIME:** 20 MINUTES

¼ cup olive oil

1 tablespoon sweet paprika

1 teaspoon ground cumin

¾ teaspoon kosher salt

¼ teaspoon freshly ground black pepper

¼ teaspoon cayenne

4 pitas, cut into 8 triangles each

Preheat the oven to 350°F. In a large bowl, combine the olive oil, paprika, cumin, salt, pepper, and cayenne. Add the pita wedges and toss to coat. Divide evenly between two baking sheets and bake, tossing once, until browned and crisp, 14 to 15 minutes (chips will harden further when removed from the oven). Cool completely before serving. Store in an airtight container for up to 1 week. To reheat, spread in a single layer on a baking sheet and bake in a 325°F oven for 7 to 8 minutes.

Hands-Off Caramelized Onion & Labaneh Dip

MAKES 2 CUPS • ACTIVE TIME: 10 MINUTES • **TOTAL TIME:** 45 MINUTES

My husband is obsessed with the classic version of onion dip, the one that mixes the Lipton packet with a tub of sour cream. It's undeniably delicious, and here's my take—just freshened up a bit. The big shortcut here is oven-roasting the onions instead of caramelizing them with the labor-intensive, traditional skillet method. The results are shockingly similar! Using labaneh instead of sour cream geotags this recipe in the Middle Eastern kitchen, and adding onion and garlic powders pays homage to my American roots. In short, a very Adeena recipe.

- 1 jumbo onion (1 pound), finely diced (3 cups)
- ¼ cup olive oil
- 1½ teaspoons kosher salt
- ½ teaspoon freshly ground black pepper
- 1 cup labaneh or Greek yogurt
- 1 teaspoon onion powder
- 1 teaspoon garlic powder
- 3 tablespoons minced chives or scallion greens, plus more for garnish
- Potato chips or crudités, for serving

Preheat the oven to 425°F. Stir together the onions, olive oil, salt, and pepper in a 9 × 13-inch baking dish. Spread evenly to cover the surface, cover with foil, and bake until the onions release their liquid and the edges begin to turn golden, 20 minutes. Uncover, stir, re-cover, and bake until the onions are lightly golden and caramelized, another 20 minutes. Remove from the oven, cool to room temperature, and transfer to a bowl. Stir in the labaneh, onion powder, and garlic powder, then stir in the chives. Chill if desired, then top with more chives. Serve with potato chips or crudités. Dip can be refrigerated in an airtight container for up to 4 days.

Carrot-Tahini-Ginger Dip/Dressing

MAKES A SCANT 2 CUPS • ACTIVE TIME: 10 MINUTES
TOTAL TIME: 15 MINUTES (PLUS CHILLING TIME)

1 medium carrot, roughly chopped

⅓ cup pure tahini paste

3 tablespoons water

3 tablespoons unseasoned rice vinegar

3 tablespoons neutral oil

2 tablespoons toasted sesame oil

2 tablespoons sugar

1½ teaspoons kosher salt, plus more for seasoning

2-inch piece fresh ginger, peeled

2 garlic cloves

Crudités of your choosing, for serving

Inspired by the iconic Japanese restaurant salad dressing—you know the one, orange in color, sweet, gingery, and practically drinkable—this dressing/dip is every bit as addictive as you would imagine. I rendered it far superior with the addition of tahini, which only enhances the traditional flavor contributed by sesame oil. The secret is to really blend until smooth and creamy; it'll hold together in the fridge well. You'll be reaching in for a spoonful every opportunity you get. It also works great as a marinade/coating/topping for roasted fish or chicken.

1. In a blender, combine the carrot, tahini, water, vinegar, neutral and sesame oils, sugar, salt, ginger, and garlic and blend on high speed until creamy and smooth, 45 seconds to 1 minute. Transfer to an airtight container and chill to thicken, 1 hour. Serve with crudités.

2. Dip will keep refrigerated in an airtight container for up to 1 week; stir before serving.

Schug & Roasted Corn Guac

MAKES 3 CUPS • ACTIVE TIME: 15 MINUTES **• TOTAL TIME:** 25 MINUTES

In this avocado-obsessed country, guacamole (or some sort of avocado salad) is a near-daily indulgence when the season is right and the fruit (yes, it's a fruit) is inexpensive at the market. Roasting sweet summer corn, then folding it into the guacamole with a simplified version of my Yemenite schug, yields a new take on the classic that you'll go crazy for. Since this does end up being somewhere between a salad and a dip, it could almost serve as a light-lunch avocado toast with some good sourdough and a slice of tomato.

2 medium ears corn, husked

2 tablespoons olive oil

1¼ teaspoons kosher salt, plus more to taste

¼ teaspoon freshly ground black pepper, plus more to taste

2 large or 3 medium avocados

1½ tablespoons freshly squeezed lime juice, plus more to taste

3 tablespoons Schug (page 17 or store-bought), plus more to taste

¼ cup finely diced red onion

Tortilla chips, for serving

1. Preheat the oven to 425°F. Cut the corn off the cobs directly onto a large rimmed baking sheet (you should have about 1½ cups). Drizzle with 1 tablespoon of the olive oil and sprinkle with ¼ teaspoon of the salt and the pepper. Roast, stirring once, until lightly golden around the edges, 12 to 13 minutes.

2. In a large bowl, mash the avocados, lime juice, schug, and the remaining 1 teaspoon salt to your desired level of chunkiness. Fold in ¾ cup of the corn and the onion, then season with more schug, lime juice, and salt to taste. Transfer to a serving bowl and top with the remaining corn. Drizzle with the remaining 1 tablespoon olive oil and season with salt and pepper to taste. If you're making this in advance, press parchment or plastic wrap onto the surface of the dip to prevent browning and refrigerate for up to 24 hours. Serve with tortilla chips.

Dilly Garlicky Eggplant Dip

MAKES 2 CUPS • ACTIVE TIME: 10 MINUTES
TOTAL TIME (INCLUDING CHILLING TIME): 1 HOUR

When it comes to dressing your salat chatzilim (eggplant dip), Israelis are either team mayo or team tahini. But why pick a side? The truth is you should have both in your arsenal, and I've chosen mayo here. It helps boost the flavor of the oven-roasted eggplant, as does the copious amount of roasted garlic, lots of crunchy scallions, and a dollop of Dijon mustard—an unconventional but effective addition.

- 2 medium eggplants (2½ pounds), halved lengthwise
- 3 tablespoons olive oil, plus more for drizzling
- 2 teaspoons kosher salt, plus more for seasoning
- 1 garlic head, papery outer layers removed
- ¼ cup mayonnaise
- Finely grated zest and juice of ½ large lemon
- ¼ cup thinly sliced scallion greens, plus more for garnish
- 2 tablespoons finely chopped dill
- 1 teaspoon Dijon mustard
- ¼ teaspoon freshly ground black pepper
- Crudités, bread, or crackers, for serving

1. Preheat the oven to 400°F. Line a baking sheet with parchment paper. Brush the cut sides of the eggplant with 2 tablespoons of the olive oil and sprinkle with 1 teaspoon of the salt. Arrange, cut side down, on the prepared baking sheet.

2. Cut off the top ¼ inch of the garlic head to expose the cloves. Place on a piece of foil and drizzle with the remaining 1 tablespoon olive oil. Seal the foil around the garlic, place on the baking sheet with the eggplant, and roast until the eggplant is slumped, the underside is deeply golden, and the garlic is tender, 35 to 40 minutes.

3. Cool slightly, then flip the eggplant and remove and discard any large clusters of seeds. Scoop out the flesh onto a cutting board (discard the skins) and squeeze the garlic and any remaining liquid onto the eggplant. Finely chop the eggplant and garlic, transfer to a medium bowl, and stir in the mayonnaise, lemon zest and juice, scallions, dill, mustard, remaining 1 teaspoon salt, and the pepper. Chill for 30 minutes, transfer to a serving bowl, drizzle with olive oil, and garnish with scallion greens. Serve with crudités, bread, or crackers.

4. Dip can be refrigerated in an airtight container for up to 4 days.

Za'atar-Marinated Feta

MAKES 1½ CUPS • ACTIVE TIME: 10 MINUTES **• TOTAL TIME:** 10 MINUTES

Like the ideal guest, this perfect little recipe is low maintenance, is a great conversation starter at cocktail hour, and asks for little but contributes a lot to an evening at your home. Simply stir tangy cubed feta (I like a Greek feta, or Israeli feta from TJ's, but your fave—or what you have on hand—will do) together with good olive oil, herbs, za'atar, and lemon zest and let the flavor-meld begin. Pile it onto little toasts, toss into pasta, or eat straight from a spoon. Oh—and unlike that party guest, this dish gets better the longer it hangs around, so make room in the fridge.

- ½ cup olive oil
- 2 tablespoons diced shallots
- 2 tablespoons thinly sliced mint leaves
- 2 tablespoons Za'atar Spice Blend (page 15 or store-bought)
- 1 tablespoon finely chopped jalapeño, preferably red
- Finely grated zest and juice of ½ small lemon
- 8 ounces feta, patted dry and cut into ½-inch cubes
- Kosher salt and freshly ground black pepper
- Crusty bread or crackers, for serving

1. In a medium bowl, whisk together the olive oil, shallots, mint, za'atar, jalapeño, and lemon zest and juice. Add the feta and gently toss to coat. Season with salt and pepper to taste. Transfer to a serving bowl and serve with bread or crackers.

2. Marinated feta can be refrigerated in an airtight container for up to 5 days; if possible, remove from the fridge 30 minutes before serving.

Baharat-Spiced Mushroom Hummus

SERVES 2 AS A MAIN COURSE, 4 AS AN APPETIZER
ACTIVE TIME: 20 MINUTES • **TOTAL TIME:** 20 MINUTES

Hummus is a plate of perfection in itself, but if you top it properly, it becomes a masterpiece. Meat, fava beans, or chickpeas are more expected toppings, but I chose mushrooms (which you do find on hummus menus, albeit less frequently) to crown my bowl. They add meatiness and substance, turning this into a winning veggie main. Baharat, with its sweet and savory mix of spices, is a great liaison between the rich base and juicy mushroom topping. Make sure to process the hummus for the full two to three minutes for maximum smoothness.

- One 15-ounce can chickpeas, drained, ¼ cup liquid reserved
- 5 garlic cloves (1 left whole, 4 thinly sliced)
- Finely grated zest and juice of 1 lemon
- ⅓ cup pure tahini paste
- 5 tablespoons olive oil, plus more for drizzling
- 2 teaspoons kosher salt, plus more for seasoning
- 1 pound assorted mushrooms (shimeji, shiitake, and button), sliced
- 1 teaspoon Baharat Spice Blend (page 15 or store-bought)
- 1 teaspoon sweet paprika
- Pinch of cayenne
- ½ cup water
- ¼ cup finely chopped parsley leaves
- Freshly ground black pepper, for seasoning
- Pitas, for serving (optional)

1. In a food processor, combine the chickpeas and reserved liquid, whole garlic clove, lemon juice, tahini, 2 tablespoons of the olive oil, and 1 teaspoon of the salt and process until smooth and creamy, 2 to 3 minutes.

2. Heat a large, dry skillet over medium-high heat for 2 minutes. Add 1 tablespoon of the olive oil, spread the mushrooms out in the pan, sprinkle with the remaining 1 teaspoon salt, and let cook, undisturbed, until the bottoms are golden and have released some liquid, 5 minutes. Stir and cook until the mushrooms are deep golden, 2 to 3 minutes. Reduce the temperature to medium-low. Using a rubber spatula or wooden spoon, push the mushrooms to one side, add the remaining 2 tablespoons olive oil, the sliced garlic, baharat, paprika, and cayenne. Cook, stirring, until fragrant, 2 minutes, then stir in the mushrooms. Add the water and cook until saucy, 3 to 4 minutes. Stir in the parsley and lemon zest.

3. Spread the hummus evenly into a shallow bowl. Use the back of a spoon to create a well in the center. Top with the mushrooms, drizzle with olive oil, and season with salt and pepper. Serve with pitas, if desired.

4. Refrigerate in an airtight container for up to 3 days.

Middle Eastern Chili Crisp

MAKES 1½ CUPS • ACTIVE TIME: 10 MINUTES **• TOTAL TIME:** 30 MINUTES

This time-honored Asian condiment feels more modern and versatile with every spoonful and drizzle. Many traditional versions call for garlic, sesame seeds, and ginger. I add whole coriander and cumin seeds; when toasted, they lend additional texture and a decidedly shukky accent. There are so many things this is good on: even just drizzling on avocado toast or eggs for breakfast, with cottage cheese or yogurt for lunch, or on basically every recipe in this book for dinner. Bonus: It lasts essentially indefinitely in the fridge (though you will finish it long before it would ever perish).

- 1 cup neutral oil
- ¼ cup sesame seeds
- 1 tablespoon minced fresh ginger
- 1 tablespoon minced garlic
- ¼ cup dried minced onion
- 3 tablespoons dried red pepper flakes or Gochugaru*
- 2 teaspoons whole coriander seeds
- 2 teaspoons whole cumin seeds
- 1 teaspoon kosher salt
- 1 tablespoon soy sauce
- 1 tablespoon sugar

1. Combine the oil, sesame seeds, ginger, and garlic in a small saucepan. Cook over medium heat, stirring occasionally, until the garlic and ginger sizzle and are fragrant and the mixture is pale golden, 2 to 3 minutes.

2. Add the onion, red pepper flakes, coriander and cumin seeds, and salt. Cook, stirring, until the onions turn golden, 2 to 3 minutes. Remove from the heat and stir in the soy sauce and sugar; the mixture will briefly bubble and sizzle. Cool to room temperature. Chili crisp can be refrigerated in an airtight container for at least 3 months.

**Gochugaru, or Korean spicy red pepper flakes, have an intense flavor and delicious, fruity spiciness. Find at Korean/Asian grocers and specialty shops.*

Michel's Sun-Dried Tomato & Olive Dipping Oil w/ Burrata

MAKES 2 CUPS • ACTIVE TIME: 20 MINUTES
TOTAL TIME (INCLUDING COOLING TIME): 2 HOURS

On Fridays, customers line up at my local gourmet shop, Bazaar, to take home a few of the house-made salads and condiments from my friend Michel Haviv's delicatessen. A former fine-dining chef who opened Bazaar during the pandemic, Michel has become an anchor of my daily shuk life. I stop in every day for a schmooze and a laugh before I head home to cook and write. He's one of the most generous people I know (he also hates compliments—sorry, Michel). That generosity extended to him sharing one of his prized secret recipes with me. So-called dipping oils have become popular lately, but this is so much more than that. When simmered in olive oil, the tomatoes and garlic meld together, and the olives add a needed brininess that gives the dish bite. Finding moist sun-dried tomatoes is key, as it helps them absorb all the other flavors in the recipe.

- 1¼ cups olive oil
- 1 packed cup (4 ounces/ 10 to 11 large or 15 small) finely chopped sun-dried tomatoes
- ½ cup roughly chopped garlic (from 1 head, about 15 cloves)
- 1 small fresh hot red chile (seeded if desired), roughly chopped (2 tablespoons)
- 1 teaspoon dried oregano or za'atar leaves
- ½ cup (2 ounces) pitted kalamata olives, halved if small, quartered if large
- 1 tablespoon olive brine (optional)
- ¼ cup packed basil leaves, torn
- ½ teaspoon kosher salt, plus more to taste
- One 8-ounce ball burrata, at room temperature
- Crusty bread, for serving

Preheat the oven to 250°F. Combine the olive oil, tomatoes, garlic, chile, and oregano in a small ovenproof dish or saucepan. Cover tightly (or seal with foil), then transfer to the oven and bake until the garlic is soft and lightly golden, 1 hour 15 minutes. Remove from the oven, uncover, mash the garlic into smaller pieces with the back of a fork, then stir in the olives, olive brine (if using), basil, and salt. Let cool to room temperature, about 30 minutes. Spoon some of the mixture into a shallow bowl, arrange the burrata in the center, and cut the top open (or tear with your hands) to release the center of the cheese into the oil. Dipping oil can be refrigerated in an airtight container for up to 2 weeks.

Crispy Feta & Cabbage Cakes

Gorgeous Green Salad w/ Labaneh-Lime Dressing

Bittersweet Persimmon, Endive & Blue Cheese Salad

Georgian-Style Salad

Caesar-y Green Beans

Celery, Blood Orange & Olive Salad

Smashed Sweet Potatoes w/ Labanehtziki & Chili Crisp

Carrot & Apple Salad w/ Light Tahini Dressing

Vegetable Salads & Sides

Crispy Feta & Cabbage Cakes

MAKES 4 FRITTERS • ACTIVE TIME: 15 MINUTES **• TOTAL TIME:** 35 MINUTES

Vegetable patties (*ketzizot* in Hebrew) are a national obsession here. Entire family meals can be built around one of the endless varieties, served with a fresh salad and often some kind of sauce or yogurt on the side. I made this mildly okonomiyaki-inspired one with cabbage, which continues to show up as one of my most versatile kitchen staples: inexpensive, ready to play with a host of other textures and flavors, and so fridge-stable you have to basically sabotage it to make it go bad. Here, ingredients you've no doubt got around are melded into juicy, crisp-edged skillet fritter with extra texture thanks to the addition of scallions and cornmeal. Dollop with labaneh or yogurt for an extra-good time.

- 1 pound green cabbage, finely shredded (7 cups)
- 1½ teaspoons kosher salt, plus more for seasoning
- 1 medium carrot, grated on the large holes of a box grater
- 6 large scallions, whites thinly sliced, greens cut into 1- to 2-inch lengths
- 1 tablespoon finely chopped jalapeño
- ¾ cup (3 ounces) crumbled feta cheese
- 3 large eggs, lightly beaten
- ½ teaspoon ground turmeric
- ½ cup (115 grams) all-purpose flour
- ¼ cup cornmeal or semolina
- 1 teaspoon baking powder
- ½ cup olive oil
- Labaneh or Greek yogurt, for serving

1. In a large bowl, combine the cabbage and salt. Use your hands to scrunch the cabbage until softened, 20 to 30 seconds. Add the carrot, scallions, jalapeño, feta, eggs, and turmeric; stir to combine. Stir in the flour, cornmeal, and baking powder.

2. Line a baking sheet with paper towels. Heat 2 tablespoons of the oil in a 9- or 10-inch cast-iron or heavy skillet over medium-high heat. Measure 2 cups of the batter; add to the skillet. Flatten gently with a spatula to form a 7-inch round (about ½ inch thick). Cook until deeply golden, 3 to 4 minutes per side. Transfer to the paper towel–lined baking sheet; repeat with the remaining oil and batter. Season with salt and serve with a dollop of labaneh. Fritters can be reheated on a baking sheet in a 325°F oven for 10 minutes.

Gorgeous Green Salad w/ Labaneh-Lime Dressing

SERVES 8 • ACTIVE TIME: 25 MINUTES • **TOTAL TIME:** 25 MINUTES

Another name for this delicious, creamy-sweet-crunchy-spicy salad could be 50 Shades of Jade. The greens meld together harmoniously with the juicy pop of grapes providing an unexpected surprise amid all those veggies. Everything gets tossed in a tangy yogurt-lime dressing, cloaking the salad in coolness. A few tips: If your Persian cukes have tough or extra-waxy skins, feel free to peel them. And slice other veggies into the salad if you like! Kohlrabi and very thinly sliced zucchini instantly come to mind.

½ cup labaneh or Greek yogurt

Finely grated zest and juice of 2 small limes (2 teaspoons zest and ¼ cup juice)

3 tablespoons olive oil

½ cup chopped parsley or mint leaves

1 teaspoon kosher salt, plus more for seasoning

¼ teaspoon freshly ground black pepper, plus more for seasoning

12 ounces green cabbage, shredded (4 packed cups)

4 medium Persian cucumbers (1 pound), 2 thinly sliced and 2 halved lengthwise and cut into 1-inch pieces

1 large avocado, diced

1¼ cups frozen shelled edamame or green peas, thawed and patted dry

⅔ cup sliced green grapes

3 scallions (green and white parts), thinly sliced

1 tablespoon chopped seeded jalapeño

In a large salad bowl, whisk the labaneh, lime zest and juice, olive oil, parsley, salt, and pepper until smooth. Add the cabbage, cucumber, avocado, edamame, grapes, scallions, and jalapeño and gently toss to coat. Season with salt and pepper to taste.

Bittersweet Persimmon, Endive & Blue Cheese Salad

SERVES 4 TO 6 • ACTIVE TIME: 15 MINUTES
TOTAL TIME (INCLUDING COOLING TIME): 15 MINUTES

- ½ cup hazelnuts
- 3 tablespoons olive oil
- 2 tablespoons balsamic vinegar
- 1 tablespoon silan (date syrup) or honey
- 2 teaspoons Dijon mustard
- ½ teaspoon kosher salt
- ⅛ teaspoon cayenne
- 2 firm Fuyu persimmons (or firm pears), thinly sliced
- 3 heads red endive (about 8 ounces), separated (or 1 small head radicchio, chopped)
- ¼ cup roughly chopped mint leaves
- 3 cups (3 ounces) lightly packed baby arugula leaves
- ⅓ cup (approximately 3 ounces) crumbled Gorgonzola or other blue cheese
- Freshly ground black pepper

Persimmon season is an exciting time in our house, and reminds me of my childhood in Palo Alto, California, where we ate them freely from a seemingly limitless supply. While I love scooping up the flesh of longer, tapered Hachiya persimmons when they ripen to a silky, pudding-like texture, for salads you can't beat crisp Fuyus, with a flavor almost reminiscent of a warm-spiced pumpkin bread. I think of this as the Jenga of salads, with endive spears and persimmons hanging in the balance among crumbles of blue cheese and shards of deeply toasted hazelnuts. Balsamic vinegar and silan form the base of a sweetish dressing with caramelly notes—a match made in heaven for the cheese and nuts.

1. Preheat the oven to 350°F. Arrange the hazelnuts on a small rimmed baking sheet; toast until fragrant, 7 to 8 minutes. Remove the skins,* cool, and coarsely chop.

2. While the nuts toast, in a small bowl or jar, whisk or shake together the olive oil, vinegar, silan, mustard, salt, and cayenne until creamy and lightened in color, 10 to 15 seconds.

3. In a large salad bowl, combine the persimmons, endive, mint, and arugula. Drizzle with the dressing and gently toss to coat. Top with the Gorgonzola and hazelnuts. Finish with pepper to taste.

** To remove the skins from hazelnuts, place the roasted nuts in a towel or fabric bag and rub vigorously.*

Georgian-Style Salad

SERVES 4 TO 6 • ACTIVE TIME: 15 MINUTES
TOTAL TIME (INCLUDING COOLING TIME): 15 MINUTES

This simple salad is often served with Georgian food; its vinegarier-than-usual dressing is a sharp contrast to Israel's lemon-centric culture. I serve it with delicious Bukharan meat-and-rice plov (pictured with the salad on page 148), where it cuts through the pilaf's richness.

- ¾ cup walnut halves
- ⅓ cup distilled white vinegar
- 2 tablespoons walnut or olive oil
- ½ teaspoon kosher salt, plus more to taste
- ½ teaspoon freshly ground black pepper, plus more to taste
- 3 large vine-ripened tomatoes, cut into chunks
- 1 small onion, chopped
- 3 medium Persian cucumbers, chopped
- ⅓ cup chopped dill

1. Preheat the oven to 350°F. Arrange the walnuts on a small rimmed baking sheet; toast until fragrant and lightly golden, 6 to 7 minutes. Cool and coarsely chop.

2. In a medium salad bowl, whisk together the vinegar, oil, salt, and pepper. Add the tomatoes, onions, cucumbers, and dill and gently toss. Before serving, fold in the walnuts; season with more salt and pepper to taste.

Caesar-y Green Beans

SERVES 4 • ACTIVE TIME: 20 MINUTES **• TOTAL TIME:** 20 MINUTES

Eyal Shani, the Israeli chef with a growing roster of restaurants around the world, inspired these bright, lemony beans, which are intentionally cooked just past al dente—all the better to soak up the tart, garlicky sauce. I gave them a Caesar-y twist by adding anchovies and parm, both to bulk up the beans and add even more punch. Serve at room temperature, or even a bit cold.

3 tablespoons plus ½ teaspoon kosher salt, plus more for seasoning

2 pounds green beans, trimmed

1 large or 2 small lemons

4 garlic cloves

3 anchovies (or 2 teaspoons anchovy paste)

¼ cup olive oil

1 cup (1½ ounces) finely grated Parmigiano Reggiano cheese

Freshly ground black pepper

In a large pot, bring 12 cups water to a boil with 3 tablespoons of the salt. Add the green beans, return to a boil, and cook until bright green and just past crisp, 3 to 4 minutes (until the beans bend easily but aren't mushy and still won't snap). Drain in a colander, run under cold water for 1 minute, then drain and dry very well on a large, clean towel. Use a Microplane to finely grate the lemon zest into a large bowl, followed by the garlic. Squeeze the lemon directly into the bowl (you should have ¼ cup juice). Use the heel of a knife to smash the anchovies into a paste on a cutting board and add to the bowl along with the remaining ½ teaspoon salt. Whisk the olive oil into the bowl in a slow stream until emulsified. Add the green beans, toss gently, then gently fold in the parm. Season with more salt and pepper to taste.

Celery, Blood Orange & Olive Salad

SERVES 4 TO 6 • ACTIVE TIME: 20 MINUTES **• TOTAL TIME:** 20 MINUTES

I think of this as a wintery salad, but you could easily whip this up any time of the year. I always look forward to seeing peak citrus appear at my regular produce vendor Gershon Rabia's stand in the shuk (see photo, page 245) during colder months. The mildly salty crunch of the celery, the tart, crimson-hued blood oranges, salty, buttery olives, and sharp radishes are visually gorgeous and—even more important—super-tasty. Pair with any grilled protein—I can already see this on the plate with the Red-Rubbed Grilled Chicken (page 120).

- 2 medium blood oranges
- 4 to 5 large celery stalks, thinly sliced on the bias (3 cups)
- 1 small red onion, halved and thinly sliced (½ cup)
- ⅔ cup (13 or 14) large pitted Castelvetrano or other green olives, quartered
- 2 small radishes, thinly sliced (use a mandoline if you have one)
- ¼ cup lightly packed mint leaves
- 1 tablespoon chopped jalapeño (seeded if desired)
- 3 tablespoons olive oil
- Finely grated zest and juice of 1 lemon (1 tablespoon zest and 3 tablespoons juice)
- ½ teaspoon kosher salt
- 1 avocado, halved and sliced
- Freshly ground black pepper

Slice off the top and bottom ends of the oranges so they can sit flat on the counter. Using a sharp knife and, starting from the top, cut away the zest and white pith beneath, leaving the flesh exposed. Cut the orange into ½-inch rounds, then halve the rounds. Add to a salad bowl along with the celery, onions, olives, radishes, mint, and jalapeño. Add the olive oil, lemon zest and juice, and salt and gently toss, then gently toss in the orange and avocado slices. Season generously with black pepper.

Roasted Sweet Potatoes w/ Labanehtziki & Chili Crisp

SERVES 4 • ACTIVE TIME: 20 MINUTES • **TOTAL TIME:** 50 MINUTES

The edges of these roasted sweet spuds get crisp and caramelized, with centers like creamy candy, and their color is a burst of happiness even in the doldrums of winter. Add a quick, crunchy labaneh tzatziki and some chili crisp (use mine or store-bought), and this is a veggie side that eats almost like a main.

- 2 large or 3 medium sweet potatoes (2 pounds; each 3 inches in diameter), scrubbed and dried
- ¼ cup plus 1 tablespoon olive oil
- 1½ teaspoons kosher salt
- ½ teaspoon freshly ground black pepper
- 1 cup labaneh or Greek yogurt, excess liquid poured off
- 1¼ cups finely diced Persian cucumber (from 3 small cucumbers)
- Finely grated zest of 1 large lemon
- 2 tablespoons thinly sliced scallion greens
- 3 to 4 tablespoons Middle Eastern Chili Crisp (page 60 or store-bought chili crisp), plus more for serving

1. Preheat the oven to 400°F. Line a large baking sheet with parchment paper. Trim the ends off the sweet potatoes and cut them into 2-inch-thick rounds (you should have 11 or 12 rounds total).

2. Arrange the sweet potatoes on the prepared baking sheet, leaving space between rounds. Drizzle with ¼ cup of the olive oil and sprinkle with 1 teaspoon of the salt and the pepper, flipping to coat both sides. Roast until the undersides of the potatoes are caramelized, 20 to 25 minutes. Remove from the oven, flip the potatoes, return to the oven, and roast until the undersides are caramelized and the potatoes can be easily pierced with a fork, another 15 to 20 minutes.

3. While the potatoes are roasting, in a medium bowl combine the labaneh and 1 cup of the cucumbers with the remaining 1 tablespoon olive oil, the lemon zest, scallions, and remaining ½ teaspoon salt.

4. Arrange the sweet potatoes on a serving dish, dollop each with a heaping tablespoon of the labanehtziki, and drizzle with the desired amount of chili crisp. Garnish with the remaining ¼ cup cucumbers and serve with extra chili crisp.

Carrot & Apple Salad w/ Light Tahini Dressing

SERVES 6 • ACTIVE TIME: 25 MINUTES **• TOTAL TIME:** 25 MINUTES

There was no one more devoted to her food processor than my late mother, Steffi. If the Cuisinart could slice a recipe into submission, I truly think she loved it even more. I can still hear the methodical sound of a cucumber, carrot, or potato being pushed through the machine's mouth, the whiny trill of the slicing itself, and the thud-thud-thud of the veggies hitting the bowl. Here the machine makes quick work of thinly slicing the carrots and apples (though by all means do it by hand if it makes you happy or you don't feel like washing the processor). I purposely created a dressing where the tahini slicks the vegetables lightly rather than thickly coating them. That way, the distinct flavors and textures in the salad have the chance to really shine.

- ⅓ cup raw pepitas (pumpkin seeds)
- 1 teaspoon olive oil
- ½ teaspoon kosher salt, plus more for seasoning
- 2 small lemons
- ¼ cup pure tahini paste
- 4 medium carrots (1 pound), peeled
- 1 large green apple, skin-on, halved and cored
- ½ cup finely chopped dill
- ½ small red onion, thinly sliced
- 1 tablespoon minced red chile (seeded if desired)
- Freshly ground black pepper

1. Preheat the oven to 350°F. Arrange the pumpkin seeds on a small rimmed baking sheet. Stir in the olive oil and season with a pinch of salt. Toast until fragrant, 6 to 7 minutes.

2. Zest and juice the lemons into a salad bowl (you should have about 1 tablespoon zest and ⅓ cup juice). Whisk in the tahini and the ½ teaspoon salt.

3. Using the thin slicing blade of a food processor, a mandoline, or a sharp knife, thinly slice the carrots and apple; transfer them to the salad bowl and gently toss with the dressing. Fold in the dill, onion, and chile.

4. Before serving, season with salt and pepper to taste and top with the pumpkin seeds.

Soup

Roasted Tomato Soup w/ Za'atar & Cheese Crostini

SERVES 4 • ACTIVE TIME: 10 MINUTES • **TOTAL TIME:** 45 MINUTES

Consider this my contribution to the grilled-cheese-and-tomato-soup pantheon. The harissa deepens the flavor of the soup, which is best made in peak tomato season. A simple toast lavished with za'atar oil, spread with herby Boursin cheese, and broiled for golden goodness tops off the soup, adding the perfect flavor and textural element.

¼ cup plus 3 tablespoons olive oil

1 teaspoon ground coriander

2½ teaspoons kosher salt, plus more to taste

3 pounds ripe, red tomatoes (such as Roma or vine-ripened), cored and halved (about 9 cups)

1 large onion, cut into 1-inch chunks

1 cup low-sodium vegetable broth

1½ tablespoons Harissa (page 15 or store-bought), plus more to taste

A 5-inch length of baguette

1 tablespoon Za'atar Spice Blend (page 15 or store-bought)

⅓ to ½ cup Boursin cheese (preferably garlic & herb flavor, from a 5-ounce package)

1. Preheat the oven to 400°F. In a small bowl, combine ¼ cup of the oil, the coriander, and 2 teaspoons of the salt. Arrange the tomatoes and onions on a baking sheet, drizzle with the spiced oil, and gently stir to coat. Roast, stirring occasionally, until the onions are soft and the tomatoes have slumped and darkened in spots, 25 to 30 minutes. Transfer the roasted vegetables and any liquid to a medium pot, add the broth and harissa, and bring to a boil over medium-high heat. Reduce the heat to medium-low, simmer for 1 to 2 minutes, and use an immersion blender (or regular blender) to blend until smooth. Season with salt to taste and cover to keep warm.

2. Arrange a rack 4 to 6 inches from the broiler; preheat the broiler. Slice the baguette into ½-inch-thick slices. In a small bowl, combine the remaining 3 tablespoons olive oil, the za'atar, and the remaining ½ teaspoon salt and brush the tops of the bread slices with the oil mixture. Top each slice with about ½ tablespoon of the cheese, brush the top of the cheese with the oil mixture, and broil until the tops are browned and the edges of the bread are deeply golden, 3 to 4 minutes. Divide the soup among bowls and serve with the toasts.

Any Veggie Soup

SERVES 8 • ACTIVE TIME: 25 MINUTES • **TOTAL TIME:** 60 MINUTES

Call it stone soup, kitchen-sink soup—call it anything you want, just make it. It's a clean-out-the-crisper-drawer kind of affair, where all your veggie halves and sundry odds and ends add up to something simple and homey. If you have a parmesan rind (the hard, dotted outer skin of a wedge of real Parmigiano Reggiano cheese) and don't mind making the soup dairy, by all means throw it in; it deepens the umami of the soup, as does the optional nutritional yeast.

- 3 tablespoons olive oil
- 1 large onion, diced
- 4 garlic cloves, minced
- 3 tablespoons tomato paste
- 1½ tablespoons sweet paprika
- ½ teaspoon ground turmeric
- 8 cups chopped mixed vegetables (such as carrots, cauliflower, mushrooms, zucchini, squash, green beans, celery, sweet potatoes)
- 1 tablespoon kosher salt, plus more to taste
- 7 cups low-sodium vegetable broth
- 1 parmesan rind or 1 tablespoon nutritional yeast (optional)
- One 15-ounce can white or other beans (kidney, garbanzo), drained and rinsed
- 2 tablespoons freshly squeezed lemon juice, plus wedges for serving
- Freshly ground black pepper
- Quick Dinner Flatbread (recipe follows), for serving

Heat the olive oil in a large pot over medium-high heat. Add the onions and cook, stirring, until lightly golden, 8 to 9 minutes. Add the garlic, tomato paste, paprika, turmeric, vegetables, and ½ tablespoon of the salt and cook, stirring occasionally, until the vegetables are softened, 7 to 8 minutes. Add the broth, parmesan rind (if using), beans, and the remaining ½ tablespoon salt, raise the heat to high, bring the soup to a boil, reduce the heat to medium-low, and cook, partially covered, until the liquid has reduced slightly and the vegetables are fully cooked, 35 minutes. Stir in the lemon juice and season with salt and pepper to taste. Serve with lemon wedges and flatbread.

Quick Dinner Flatbread

MAKES 6 FLATBREADS • ACTIVE TIME: 18 MINUTES
TOTAL TIME: 30 MINUTES

The best thing about these—other than their pliability, tenderness, and slightly biscuity flavor—is how quickly and easily they come together. Somewhere between an Indian naan and a flat pita, these fluffy rounds enhance any soup they're served with, service any dip that needs a vehicle to your mouth, and graciously step up for any open-faced sandwich duty. Yogurt and olive oil enrich the dough, and baking powder gives it the proper lift, adding a drop of crispness to the proceedings.

2 cups (260 grams) all-purpose flour, plus more as needed

2 teaspoons (10 grams) baking powder

1 teaspoon (6 grams) kosher salt, plus more to taste

1 cup (280 grams) full-fat yogurt or dairy-free yogurt

2 tablespoons (26 grams) olive oil, plus 3 tablespoons for greasing the skillet

1. In a large bowl, stir together the flour, baking powder, and salt to combine. Stir in the yogurt and the 2 tablespoons olive oil, mixing until loosely combined. Turn the mixture onto a lightly floured surface and knead the dough until soft and smooth, 3 to 4 minutes, adding flour a little at a time as needed. Rest the dough, covered, until softened slightly, 10 minutes.

2. On a lightly floured surface, divide the dough into 6 equal pieces. Roll or flatten each piece with a rolling pin or by hand into a 5- to 6-inch round (about ¼ inch thick), adding more flour as needed to prevent sticking. Heat a 12-inch heavy skillet over medium-high heat. Just before cooking, brush the surface of the skillet with 1 tablespoon of olive oil. Gently transfer 2 flatbreads to the skillet and cook until puffed and golden brown, 2 to 3 minutes per side. Repeat with the remaining olive oil and dough rounds, covering the cooked breads to keep warm. Season with more salt to taste. Extra flatbreads can be tightly wrapped and frozen, then unwrapped, wrapped in a clean kitchen towel, and microwaved in 30-second intervals until soft and warm.

Tart Chicken Meatball & Greens Soup (Hamusta)

SERVES 6 • ACTIVE TIME: ABOUT 30 MINUTES **• TOTAL TIME:** 1 HOUR

This was the first (!) recipe I developed for this book, so I love it not only for sentimental reasons but because it's a delicious spin on my favorite Iraqi-Kurdish soup, kubbeh hamusta. It's typically a homey bowl of semolina-wrapped beef meatballs swimming in a lemony broth strewn with wilted greens, but I swapped in tender chicken meatballs instead for ease. The rice in the meatballs keeps them tender (and gluten-free), and the whole thing comes together in around 30 minutes' active time. (See photo, p. 82.)

½ cup long-grain rice, such as basmati or jasmine

2 medium onions

1½ pounds ground chicken (preferably a combination of light and dark meat)

1 cup packed parsley leaves, finely chopped (⅓ cup)

1 large egg, beaten

Finely grated zest and juice of 2 lemons (4 teaspoons zest and 6 tablespoons juice), plus more juice if desired

6 tablespoons olive oil, plus more for oiling your hands

2 tablespoons kosher salt, plus more to taste

1 large bunch Swiss chard (1¼ pounds), whites and greens thinly sliced

8 cups low-sodium chicken broth

2 teaspoons ground turmeric

2 tablespoons sliced jalapeño

2 cups water

One 15-ounce can chickpeas, drained

2 medium zucchini, cut into ½-inch rounds

1. Place the rice in a bowl and cover with 3 inches hot tap water. Soak for 10 minutes and drain well. Grate one of the onions on the large holes of a box grater into a large bowl (thinly slice the second onion and reserve). Add the chicken, rice, parsley, egg, 1 tablespoon of the lemon zest, 2 tablespoons of the olive oil, and 1 tablespoon of the salt to the grated onion. Use oiled hands to gently mix all the ingredients until incorporated.

2. Heat the remaining ¼ cup olive oil in a large pot over medium heat. Add the sliced onions, half the chard leaves and stems, and a splash of broth. Cook, stirring, until wilted, 2 to 3 minutes. Add the rest of the chard and continue to cook, stirring, until the onions are translucent and the greens have reduced in size, 5 to 6 minutes. Stir in the turmeric and jalapeño, then add the remaining broth, the water, chickpeas, zucchini, and remaining 1 tablespoon salt. Raise the heat to high and bring the soup to a boil. Use oiled hands to form the meat mixture (mixture will be loose, not firm) into 12 equal-sized meatballs and gently lower the meatballs into the soup as you shape them. Return the pot to a boil, reduce the heat to medium-low, and simmer until the meatballs are cooked through, 30 to 35 minutes. Stir in the lemon juice and the remaining zest, then season to taste with more lemon juice, salt, and jalapeño.

Garlicky Semolina Porridge (Chashu)

SERVES 4 TO 6 • ACTIVE TIME: 15 MINUTES **• TOTAL TIME:** 20 MINUTES

From the moment it opened in 2022 until it closed last summer, I was entranced with Bottarga, a tiny restaurant stall at the top of the Carmel Market that was run by now-twenty-six-year-old Priel Shabo. In the winter months you'd find me there often, partaking of her steaming bowls of kubbeh soup, meatballs, root vegetable stew, crisp market salads, and a garlicky semolina porridge called chashu. The chashu was so delicious that I invited Priel over to my house to teach me how to make it. With her Moroccan grandmother on speakerphone for guidance, she quickly set to work chopping a raft of garlic, sautéing it until fragrant, then added water and salt. She streamed in semolina a little at a time, stirring as the mixture thickened into a sort of loose, soupy polenta. After adding a generous amount of cilantro, she ladled me a bowl, and it was one of the most inexpensive, and delicious, lunches I'd ever had.

⅓ cup olive oil

9 garlic cloves, finely minced

1½ teaspoons ground turmeric

1 teaspoon coarsely ground black pepper

9 cups water

2 tablespoons kosher salt, plus more to taste

1¼ cups (250 grams) coarsely ground semolina

1 large bunch cilantro, finely chopped (2 cups)

Lemon wedges, for serving

Toasted bread, for serving

Heat the olive oil in a large pot over medium-low heat. Add the garlic and cook, stirring, until fragrant but still pale, 2 minutes. Add the turmeric and pepper and cook, stirring, until fragrant, 1 minute. Add the water and salt, raise the heat to high, and bring to a boil. Reduce the heat to medium and add the semolina in a slow, steady stream, whisking constantly. Continue to whisk, stirring, until the liquid has thickened to the texture of cake batter, 2 to 3 minutes from the time it comes to a boil. Stir in the cilantro and season with more salt to taste. Divide among bowls and serve with lemon wedges and bread. The soup will thicken to an almost polenta-like texture when cooled or chilled; to thin, add hot water while reheating until you achieve your desired thinness.

Chilled Basil-Lime Pea Soup

SERVES 4 AS A MAIN COURSE, 6 AS AN APPETIZER
ACTIVE TIME: 10 MINUTES
TOTAL TIME (INCLUDING CHILLING TIME): 2 HOURS 30 MINUTES

I can think of many ways I'd rather spend time than the two hours it would take to shell 4 cups of fresh peas, and besides—frozen work great here (not to mention they're one of my husband Jay's nostalgic favorites from childhood). Cashews really are a great way to add creaminess without cream, and though this is advertised as a chilled soup, good news for the impatient: It tastes great hot, too.

3 tablespoons olive oil

1 large onion, diced

3 garlic cloves, minced

4 cups low-sodium vegetable broth or water

⅔ cup raw cashews

2½ teaspoons kosher salt, plus more to taste

4 cups frozen peas (not thawed)

¾ cup lightly packed basil leaves, plus more sliced for garnish

Finely grated zest and juice of 1 lime, plus lime halves for serving

Roasted, salted cashews, for serving (optional)

Heat the olive oil in a medium saucepan over medium heat. Add the onions and cook, stirring, until lightly golden, 8 to 9 minutes. Add the garlic and cook, stirring, 1 more minute. Add the broth, cashews, and salt. Bring to a boil, reduce the heat to medium-low, and simmer until the cashews soften slightly, 5 minutes. Add the peas, turn off the heat, and let sit until the peas are tender, 6 to 7 minutes. Cool slightly, transfer to a blender (you can also use an immersion blender, though it will be slightly less smooth), add the basil, and blend until very smooth, 2 minutes. Transfer to a bowl, cover partially (this allows for faster cooling) and refrigerate until chilled, at least 2 hours. Uncover, thin slightly with water if needed, then add the lime zest and juice, season with salt to taste, and divide among bowls. Garnish with more basil and the roasted cashews (if using). Serve with lime halves.

Creamy Corn & Cod Chowder

SERVES 4 TO 6 AS A MAIN COURSE, 8 AS AN APPETIZER
ACTIVE TIME: 25 MINUTES • **TOTAL TIME:** 50 MINUTES

My maternal grandmother, Ann Nadrich, hated to cook, and when my grandfather retired from his restaurant-supply business, she said she retired, too—from the kitchen. They happily ate out both lunch and dinner for decades, though once a year she made delicious potato latkes, which she would serve with a corn "chowder" consisting of little more than milk and canned corn. Grandma, this one's for you. I upgraded the recipe with a rich, creamy base—easily made dairy-free by swapping in milk substitutes—studded with potatoes, corn, and celery, plus chunks of fish you add at the very end. Work ahead by making the soup base, then reheat and add the fish. This may be one of the least Middle Eastern-inspired dishes in the book, but it's hands-down a crowd favorite in any country.

- 3 tablespoons olive oil
- 1 large onion, diced
- 3 large celery stalks, diced
- 2 garlic cloves, minced
- 1 tablespoon chopped jalapeño, plus more for garnish
- 3 cups low-sodium vegetable broth or water
- Two 15-ounce cans corn (preferably with no added sugar), not drained*
- 1 large potato (about 12 ounces), peeled and cut into ¾-inch pieces
- 1½ cups whole milk (or barista-style plant-based milk of your choice)
- ½ cup heavy cream (or full-fat coconut milk)
- 1 tablespoon kosher salt, plus more to taste
- ¼ teaspoon freshly ground black pepper, plus more to taste
- 1½ pounds skinless whitefish fillets, such as cod, cut into 2-inch chunks
- Crusty bread, for serving

1. Heat the olive oil in a large pot over medium-high heat. Add the onions and celery and cook, stirring, until they start to soften, 5 minutes. Add the garlic and jalapeño and cook, stirring, until softened, 2 minutes. Add the broth, the cans of corn and their liquid, and the potatoes, bring to a boil, reduce the heat to medium-low, and simmer, partially covered, until the potatoes are tender, 15 to 16 minutes.

2. Stir in the milk, cream, salt, and pepper; return to a simmer. Use an immersion blender to blend the soup until some of the liquid is creamy but some chunks of potato and most of the corn kernels remain, 15 to 20 seconds. Add the fish; simmer until opaque and flaky, 5 minutes. Season with salt and pepper, garnish with jalapeño, and divide among bowls. Serve with bread.

**To use fresh corn, cut the kernels off 3 large ears corn. To use frozen corn, use 3½ cups frozen corn kernels. In both cases, add 1¾ additional cups vegetable broth or water.*

Smoky Split Pea & Freekeh Soup

SERVES 8 • ACTIVE TIME: 20 MINUTES
TOTAL TIME: 2 HOURS 45 MINUTES (OR MORE AS NEEDED)

My mom usually got her split pea soup going with a sleeve of Manischewitz soup starter (I miss them!), which contained legumes and spices in a plastic tube. She'd add sliced-up hot dogs and more barley to round out the dish, turning it into a meal. My version is laced through with pastrami, seasoned with smoked paprika, and made extra special with the use of freekeh, the ancient grain referred to in the Old Testament and harvested here every year by Palestinian farmers, who smoke it over wood for a unique, delicious flavor. So that's three smoky, yet not overwhelming, elements in one bowl. Remember to have patience, as the peas will take a full 2 hours (or more) to soften. If you don't have pastrami, swap in salami, hot dogs, smoked sausage, or whatever flavorful cured meat you've got around.

- ¼ cup olive oil
- 2 medium carrots, cut into ¼-inch-thick half-moons (2 cups)
- 3 large celery stalks, diced (1¼ cups)
- 1 medium onion, diced
- 1½ cups dried green or yellow split peas, picked through
- ⅔ cup freekeh*
- 6 cups low-sodium beef broth (or water)
- 6 cups water
- 1 bay leaf
- 1 tablespoon smoked paprika
- 8 ounces pastrami or other smoked cured meat, diced
- 4 teaspoons kosher salt, plus more to taste
- ½ teaspoon freshly ground black pepper, plus more to taste
- Baguette slices, for serving

Heat the olive oil in a large pot over medium-high heat. Add the carrots, celery, and onions and cook, stirring, until the onions are translucent, 7 minutes. Add the split peas, freekeh, broth, water, and bay leaf, raise the heat to high, and skim any scum off the soup as it comes to a boil. Reduce the heat to medium-low, add the paprika, and simmer, covered, stirring occasionally, until the soup gets cloudy and the freekeh has softened, 1 hour. Uncover, add the pastrami, re-cover, and simmer, stirring occasionally, until the peas soften completely and the soup has thickened, 2 to 3 hours. Stir in the salt and pepper, seasoning with more of each to taste. Divide among bowls. (When reheating leftovers, you may need to add more water to thin out the soup.) Serve with baguette slices.

**If you can't find freekeh, use pearled barley, wheatberries, or farro (you may need slightly more water; adjust as necessary).*

Marak Lavan (White Root Vegetable Soup)

SERVES 8 • ACTIVE TIME: 20 MINUTES **• TOTAL TIME:** 1 HOUR 15 MINUTES

Thousands of you have made the Marak Katom (orange soup) from *Sababa*, a recipe in which a combination of like-minded (or at least -hued) veggies are simmered with alliums in liquid before being pureed to silky, soupy perfection. I took that concept and ran with it to create this paler (but no less wonderful) rendition. Diced pear lends sweetness in lieu of more conventional sweeteners, and the roasted pine nuts add crunch and a bit of luxury to the top. Velvet in a bowl. This one freezes like a dream!

- ⅓ cup olive oil, plus more for drizzling
- 1 medium onion, diced
- 2 garlic cloves
- 2 teaspoons kosher salt, plus more to taste
- 8 cups chopped white vegetables (celery root, parsnips, cauliflower, potatoes), about 2½ pounds
- 1 medium pear, peeled, cored, and chopped
- 5 cups vegetable broth, plus more as needed
- ¼ teaspoon white pepper
- ⅓ cup pine nuts
- Finely grated zest of 1 medium lemon

1. Heat the olive oil in a large pot over medium heat. Add the onions, garlic, and ¼ teaspoon of the salt and cook, stirring, until the onions are lightly golden, 8 to 9 minutes. Add the vegetables, pears, and another ½ teaspoon of the salt and cook, stirring, until the vegetables begin to soften, 5 to 6 minutes. Add the broth and white pepper, bring to a boil, then reduce the heat to low and simmer, partially covered, until the vegetables are completely tender, 30 to 35 minutes.

2. While the soup is simmering, preheat the oven to 350°F. Arrange the pine nuts on a small rimmed baking sheet; stir with a bit of olive oil and toast until lightly golden, 7 to 8 minutes. When the soup is ready, use an immersion blender to blend the soup directly in the pot until smooth, 2 to 3 minutes (or transfer to a blender in batches and blend on high speed until creamy, 1 to 2 minutes). Stir in the remaining 1¼ teaspoons salt and the lemon zest. Season with more salt to taste, divide among bowls, garnish with pine nuts, and drizzle with olive oil.

Fish

Crisp-Skinned Fish w/ Watermelon, Tomato & Cucumber Salad
Mustard-Sumac Salmon w/ Citrus-Beet Salad
Harissa Butter Roasted Fish w/ Corn, Tomato, Avo & Feta Salad
Fig & Yellowtail Crudo w/ Spicy Labaneh
Sheet Pan Amba-Glazed Fish w/ Snow Peas
Carmel Market Fish Sandwiches
B'stila-Inspired Salmon

Crisp-Skinned Fish w/ Watermelon, Tomato & Cucumber Salad

SERVES 4 • ACTIVE TIME: 20 MINUTES **• TOTAL TIME:** 20 MINUTES

This past summer in Tel Aviv was one of back-to-back 90-degree, 70 percent humidity days—for weeks at a time. Dips in the nearby sea and sticking my head in the freezer helped, but so did recipes like this one, where the only heat involved was quickly cooking the fish on the stovetop (pat the fish really dry before cooking). All the vegetables are at their peak in the warmer months, and they really shine when combined in a gazpacho-vibed salad dressed with tart vinegar, grassy olive oil, and shreds of mint, the dregs of which you'll want to tip into your mouth straight from the bowl. You can also serve the salad on its own, or as an accompaniment to other dishes in the book, such as the Spice-Drawer Schnitzel on page 124 and on the book's cover.

- One 10-ounce piece of rindless watermelon, cut into ½-inch cubes (2 cups)
- 2 medium vine-ripened tomatoes, cut into ½-inch cubes
- 3 medium Persian cucumbers, cut into ½-inch cubes
- ½ cup finely diced red onion
- 1 tablespoon finely diced jalapeño, plus more to taste
- 3 tablespoons finely shredded mint, plus more for garnish
- 5 tablespoons olive oil, plus more for serving
- 3 tablespoons sherry vinegar, white balsamic vinegar, or white wine vinegar
- ½ teaspoon kosher salt, plus more for seasoning
- ¼ teaspoon freshly ground black pepper, plus more for seasoning
- Four 6-ounce skin-on whitefish fillets, such as sea bass or branzino

1. In a large bowl, combine the watermelon, tomatoes, cucumbers, onions, jalapeño, and mint. Add 3 tablespoons of the olive oil, the vinegar, salt, and pepper; gently toss.

2. Pat the fish dry; season the skin side generously with salt. Heat a large (10-inch) dry nonstick skillet over medium-high heat until very hot, 2 to 3 minutes. Add 1 tablespoon of the olive oil, then 2 fillets, skin side down, and cook, pressing down often with a spatula, until the edges underneath are deep golden and the underside is crisp, 3 minutes. Season the tops with salt, then flip and cook until the fish is just cooked through, 1 to 2 more minutes. Wipe out the pan, then repeat with the remaining 1 tablespoon olive oil and 2 fillets. Divide most of the salad and juices among four wide, shallow bowls, then top each bowl with a fish fillet, skin side up. Spoon a little of the remaining salad on top of each bowl, if desired, then drizzle with olive oil and garnish with mint.

Mustard-Sumac Salmon w/ Citrus-Beet Salad

SERVES 4 • ACTIVE TIME: 20 MINUTES **• TOTAL TIME:** 40 MINUTES

Sumac, which grows wild in these parts come springtime, is harvested by hand, then dried and crushed into a chunky spice that enhances everything it touches. Beware of sumac that's too bright-pink in color; chances are it had some artificial help! Here, along with mustard and lemon, sumac adds tang and color to this dish. The topping cloaks the fish like a tailored suit, helping it remain perfectly tender and flaky nestled into a bed of citrus, beets, and greens.

2 to 3 medium beets (1 pound),* peeled and cut into ½-inch cubes

5 tablespoons olive oil

1½ teaspoons kosher salt

1¼ teaspoons freshly ground black pepper

¾ cup walnut halves, coarsely chopped

Four 6-ounce skin-on, center-cut salmon fillets

4 tablespoons grainy Dijon mustard

3 tablespoons light brown sugar

Finely grated zest and juice of 1 lemon

1 tablespoon plus 1 teaspoon ground sumac

8 cups (10 ounces) lightly packed baby arugula leaves

1 small red onion, thinly sliced

½ cup pomegranate seeds

1 pink grapefruit, rind and white pith removed, sliced into thin rounds, quartered

1. Arrange two racks in the top and center of the oven; preheat to 425°F. Arrange the beets on a large parchment-lined baking sheet. Toss with 1 tablespoon of the olive oil, ½ teaspoon of the salt, and ¼ teaspoon of the pepper; roast on the center rack, stirring once, until softened and slightly shriveled, 25 to 30 minutes. Arrange the walnuts on a small baking sheet. Arrange the salmon on a medium parchment-lined baking sheet; season with ½ teaspoon each of the salt and pepper. In a small bowl, combine 3 tablespoons of the mustard, 2 tablespoons of the brown sugar, the lemon zest, 1 tablespoon of the sumac, and ¼ teaspoon each of the salt and pepper. Spread 2 tablespoons of the mustard mixture on top of each salmon fillet. During the last 10 minutes of the beets roasting, roast the salmon and walnuts on the top rack until the nuts are fragrant and the salmon is just cooked through, 5 minutes for the walnuts and 8 to 9 minutes for the salmon.

2. In a bowl, whisk the lemon juice with the remaining 4 tablespoons olive oil, 1 tablespoon mustard, 1 tablespoon brown sugar, 1 teaspoon sumac, and ¼ teaspoon each salt and pepper. In a large bowl, toss the arugula, beets, onions, walnuts, and pomegranate seeds with the dressing. Divide the greens and grapefruit slices among four plates; top each with a salmon fillet (leave the skin behind if you wish).

**Swap fresh beets for two 8-ounce packages vacuum-sealed cooked beets. Pat dry, quarter, and proceed with the instructions.*

Harissa Butter Roasted Fish w/ Corn, Tomato, Avo & Feta Salad

SERVES 4 TO 5 • ACTIVE TIME: 20 MINUTES • **TOTAL TIME:** 30 MINUTES

Along with Yemenite schug, harissa ties for first as *the* hot sauce of our home. It's got notes of paprika, hot peppers, and garlic in every spoonful without a lot of vinegary bite, making it a balanced, flavor-packed pantry staple. Here, I combine it with butter and even more garlic to make a compound butter that tops the fish with richness and heat. The accompanying salad, with its fresh market produce and za'atar dressing, would be good as a side dish or light lunch on its own.

- ½ stick (4 tablespoons) unsalted butter, softened
- 1 tablespoon Harissa (page 15 or store-bought)
- 1 large garlic clove, finely minced
- 1 teaspoon kosher salt, plus more for seasoning
- ½ teaspoon freshly ground black pepper
- Four or five 5- to 6-ounce skinless whitefish fillets, such as sea bass or snapper
- 2 large ears corn, husked*
- 12 ounces (2½ cups) cherry tomatoes, quartered
- 2 tablespoons Za'atar Spice Blend (page 15 or store-bought)
- 3 tablespoons finely chopped chives
- 2 tablespoons finely chopped jalapeño
- 3 tablespoons freshly squeezed lemon juice
- 3 tablespoons olive oil
- 1 large firm but ripe avocado, finely diced
- ½ cup (2 ounces) crumbled feta cheese

1. Arrange a rack in the center of the oven; preheat to 375°F.

2. In a shallow bowl, combine the butter, harissa, garlic, ½ teaspoon of the salt, and ¼ teaspoon of the pepper and mash with a fork until smooth. Arrange the fish in a 10-inch round or square baking dish; pat the fish dry. Season lightly with salt and pepper and spread each fillet with 1 tablespoon of the harissa butter, adding any extra butter to the baking dish. Roast, using a spoon to baste with the melted harissa butter once midway through, until the fish is opaque and the butter is bubbly, 12 to 13 minutes. Remove from the oven, baste again with the melted butter, and season with more salt.

3. While the fish is roasting, cut the corn off the cobs into a medium bowl; you should have about 2 generous cups. Add the tomatoes, za'atar, chives, jalapeño, lemon juice, olive oil, and the remaining ½ teaspoon salt and ¼ teaspoon pepper; gently toss to coat. Gently fold in the avocado and feta before serving. Serve the salad with the fish.

**You can also use 2 cups drained canned corn or 2¼ cups frozen, thawed, and drained corn kernels.*

Fig & Yellowtail Crudo w/ Spicy Labaneh

SERVES 4 • ACTIVE TIME: 15 MINUTES **• TOTAL TIME:** 15 MINUTES

In the fall there's a very short local yellowtail fishing season. When it comes, restaurants do little more than slice the catch into pristine ingots of clean-tasting, oceany fish. Here, I pair the fish with juicy figs and a bed of spicy, tangy labaneh that provides the perfect counterbalance to the sweetness of the figs and the richness of the fish. Of course, swap in other fruit (mango comes to mind) and fish; tuna or salmon would be wonderful here. Though you can slice it yourself, a fishmonger—and, these days, many supermarkets—may offer it presliced and ready to use.

- 1 medium jalapeño
- 1 lemon, halved
- 1 cup labaneh or Greek yogurt
- 4 tablespoons olive oil
- 2 tablespoons chopped cilantro leaves, plus more leaves for garnish
- ½ teaspoon kosher salt
- 8 ounces sushi-grade yellowtail (or tuna or salmon), thinly sliced
- 4 or 5 figs, thinly sliced
- Flaky sea salt, for garnish

Slice about 10 thin rings off the jalapeño, then halve and seed the rest of the pepper and finely chop it. Squeeze half the lemon into a medium bowl, then whisk the labaneh, 2 tablespoons of the olive oil, the chopped cilantro, 1 tablespoon (or a bit less or more) of the chopped jalapeño, and the kosher salt. Spread the labaneh on a large (at least dinner-plate-sized) platter, then arrange the fish and figs on top in any pattern you want. Zest and juice the other half of the lemon into a small bowl, then whisk in the remaining 2 tablespoons olive oil. Drizzle over the platter, top with the reserved jalapeño rings and cilantro leaves, and garnish with flaky salt.

Sheet Pan Amba-Glazed Fish w/ Snow Peas

SERVES 4 • ACTIVE TIME: 10 MINUTES **• TOTAL TIME:** 20 MINUTES

The biggest obstacle to making this incredible recipe is finding amba—a funky, punchy condiment with a hint of ferment—itself. There's an easy recipe for this in the Staples section of this book (see page 14), and there are also good jarred versions for sale online (and at kosher stores; see Shopping, page 10). Alternatively, you can buy some Indian green mango pickle, blend it a bit, and swap that in. For a simple, one-pan fish dinner, I incorporate the amba into a sweet-tangy glaze, then scatter snow peas all around the fish before roasting everything together. Trimmed green beans work very well here, too, if you have those on hand.

- 1 pound snow peas, threaded (or trimmed green beans, left whole)
- 5 tablespoons olive oil
- ½ teaspoon kosher salt, plus more to taste
- Freshly ground black pepper
- 2 tablespoons Amba (page 14 or store-bought)
- 3 tablespoons finely chopped cilantro, plus more for garnish
- 2 tablespoons light brown sugar
- Four 6-ounce skin-on whitefish fillets (such as sea bass or sole), patted dry

1. Arrange a rack in the top third of the oven; preheat to 425°F. Line a large baking sheet with parchment paper.

2. Arrange the peas on the prepared baking sheet, drizzle with 2 tablespoons of the olive oil, season with ¼ teaspoon of the salt and pepper to taste, and toss to coat. In a small bowl, whisk the amba, cilantro, brown sugar, remaining 3 tablespoons olive oil, and remaining ¼ teaspoon salt. Season the fish with salt and pepper, nestle it among the peas, and brush about 1 tablespoon of the amba mixture on each fillet. Place the fish on the top rack and roast until the fish is almost cooked, 4 to 5 minutes. Remove from the oven, preheat the broiler, return to the oven, and broil until the glaze darkens slightly and begins to bubble and the peas are crisp-tender, 2 to 3 minutes. Serve the fish with the peas; garnish with cilantro.

Carmel Market Fish Sandwiches

MAKES 2 SANDWICHES • ACTIVE TIME: 20 MINUTES
TOTAL TIME: 25 MINUTES

Just inside the Carmel Market sits Hacarmel 40, a tiny stall that sells the best fish sandwich in the world. One reason? The Israeli chef, Elad Amitai, procures his fish from Rustum Mansour, an Arab fishmonger whose shop sits directly behind the stall. Every day you'll see Elad's staff hollowing out bread to house the ultimate fixings: a day-catch fish fillet seared on a flat top, then layered with shredded lettuce and a variety of sauces and herbs. I simplified the recipe by roasting the fish in the oven and condensing the flavors into one sauce (the secret ingredient: pickled pepperoncini peppers!) for which you'll find multiple uses.

- 1 cup picked parsley or cilantro leaves (or a combination)
- ⅓ cup plus 2 tablespoons olive oil
- 3 tablespoons freshly squeezed lemon juice
- 3 tablespoons drained sliced pickled pepperoncini peppers
- 2 garlic cloves (plus 1 more, if desired)
- ½ teaspoon kosher salt, plus more for seasoning
- 2 ciabatta or other crusty sandwich rolls, split
- Two 6-ounce skin-on fish fillets, such as sea bass, patted dry
- Freshly ground black pepper
- 2 tablespoons mayonnaise
- 1 cup shredded romaine lettuce
- ½ cup sliced red onion
- 1 tomato, thinly sliced

1. In a blender, combine the herbs with ⅓ cup of the olive oil, the lemon juice, pepperoncini, garlic, and salt. Blend until creamy, 30 seconds (you should have about ⅔ cup sauce). Sauce will keep, refrigerated, in an airtight container for 2 weeks.

2. Arrange a rack 4 inches from the broiler; preheat the broiler. Arrange the bread on a small rimmed baking sheet and brush the inside of each roll with ½ tablespoon of the olive oil. Arrange the fish on another small rimmed baking sheet and brush both sides of the fish with the remaining 1 tablespoon olive oil, ending with the skin side up. Season the rolls and fish with salt and pepper. Broil the fish until the skin puffs and turns golden and the fish is cooked, 6 to 7 minutes.

3. During the last 2 minutes of broiling the fish, add the rolls to the rack and broil until golden, 1 to 2 minutes. Spread 1 tablespoon of the mayonnaise on each roll, then top the bottom half of each roll with half of the lettuce and onions, and drizzle 2 tablespoons of the green sauce on top of the lettuce. Top with a fish fillet, followed by the tomato slices. Drizzle with more sauce, close the sandwiches, and cut in half with a serrated knife. Serve with the remaining sauce.

B'stila-Inspired Salmon

SERVES 5 TO 6 • ACTIVE TIME: 10 MINUTES **• TOTAL TIME:** 30 MINUTES

SHOWSTOPPER ALERT! This is my *very* loose, gorgeous, and irresistible interpretation of a Moroccan classic. Traditionally, chicken (or pigeon) is mixed with aromatics, herbs, dates, almonds, and warm spices, all wrapped in a flaky phyllo pastry. For my version I borrowed the top-note flavor profile of the original and cloaked salmon in a similarly inspired mixture, transforming a whole fillet into a dish worthy of a dinner party (or weeknight) with minimal work. I'm always learning new things about dishes I've been making for years; here, I discovered that coating Medjool dates in a bit of oil before chopping helps them slide off the knife with ease. Serve with salad and couscous to make this a complete meal.

4 large or 6 small pitted Medjool dates (4 ounces), halved

3 tablespoons olive oil, plus more for the dates and oiling your hands

⅔ cup slivered almonds

½ cup chopped mint, plus more for garnish

2 tablespoons finely minced jalapeño (preferably red) or ½ teaspoon dried red pepper flakes

1½ teaspoons ground cumin

1 teaspoon kosher salt, plus more for seasoning the fish

½ teaspoon ground cinnamon

One 2½-pound skin-on salmon fillet, patted dry

Freshly ground black pepper

2 tablespoons silan (date syrup) or honey

1 lemon

Salad and couscous, for serving

Preheat the oven to 400°F. Line a rimmed baking sheet or large rectangular baking dish with parchment paper (this is optional; it will just make cleanup easier). Arrange the dates on a cutting board and rub them all over with a bit of olive oil (this makes them easier to cut). Thinly slice the date halves (you should have a scant ½ cup). Transfer to a small bowl and toss with the olive oil, almonds, mint, jalapeño, cumin, salt, and cinnamon. Arrange the salmon on the prepared baking sheet and season with salt and pepper. Brush the silan on the salmon and use lightly oiled hands to spread the almond-date mixture all over the top. Roast until the almonds are lightly golden, the dates are caramelized, and the salmon is medium-rare in the center (120°F if you are using a thermometer), 13 to 14 minutes. Remove from the oven, zest the lemon right on top, halve the lemon, squeeze onto the salmon before serving, and garnish with more mint. Serve with salad and couscous, if desired.

Poultry

Tomatoey Skillet Eggplant Chicken Thighs

Red-Rubbed Grilled Chicken w/ Pom-Cauli Tabbouleh

Za'atar-Honey Chicken Wings w/ Spicy Tahini Dipping Sauce

Spice-Drawer Schnitzel w/ Pickle Mayo Sauce

Sheet Pan Chermoula Chicken w/ Red Cabbage & Sweet Potatoes

Deli Salad–Topped Grilled Chicken

Toum-ish Chicken Thighs w/ Roasted Radishes, Apples & Fennel

Simple Rotisserie-Style Chicken

Shawarma-Spiced Turkey Pita Smashburgers

One-Pan Chicken Drumstick Tagine

Sheet Pan Shipudim (Skewers) w/ Za'atar Potato Wedges

Tomatoey Skillet Eggplant Chicken Thighs

SERVES 6 • ACTIVE TIME: 20 MINUTES **• TOTAL TIME:** 1 HOUR 10 MINUTES

In this single-skillet recipe, I opted to brown the eggplant—typically a labor-intensive, splattery endeavor—in the oven, and I was delighted with the results: so much golden goodness, none of the mess. This umami-packed recipe gets a triple dose of tomatoes from fresh, sun-dried, *and* tomato paste, all of which boost and concentrate flavor. Once everything is roasted together, you get juicy chicken, silky eggplant, and jammy tomatoes in every bite.

- One 1¼-pound eggplant, cut into 2-inch-thick chunks
- ½ cup olive oil
- 3 teaspoons kosher salt, plus more to taste
- ½ cup water
- 3 tablespoons silan (date syrup) or honey
- 2 tablespoons tomato paste
- 1 tablespoon sweet paprika
- ½ teaspoon ground cumin
- ¼ teaspoon dried red pepper flakes
- ½ teaspoon freshly ground black pepper
- 4 small or 3 medium Roma tomatoes, halved
- 10 garlic cloves, sliced
- 4 sun-dried tomatoes, thinly sliced (¼ cup)
- Six 5-ounce boneless, skinless chicken thighs (pargiyot; 2 pounds total)
- Cooked couscous or rice, for serving

1. Preheat the oven to 450°F. Arrange the eggplant in a large (12-inch) ovenproof heavy skillet with a lid. Toss with the oil, then ½ teaspoon of the salt, to coat. Roast, uncovered, until the eggplant is golden in parts and tender, 15 minutes.

2. While the eggplant is roasting, in a medium bowl, combine the water, 1½ tablespoons of the silan, the tomato paste, paprika, 1 teaspoon of the salt, the cumin, and red pepper flakes. Season the chicken all over with the remaining 1½ teaspoons salt and the pepper.

3. Remove the skillet from the oven (make sure to use oven mitts); reduce the temperature to 425°F. Nestle the tomatoes among the eggplant pieces and scatter the garlic and sun-dried tomatoes on top.

4. Arrange the chicken on top of the vegetables, stir the liquid, pour it over the chicken, tilt to distribute evenly, cover, transfer to the oven, and bake until the liquid is bubbly and the tomatoes have begun to soften, 25 minutes. Uncover, brush the chicken with the remaining 1½ tablespoons silan, and roast until the sauce reduces, the eggplant is soft, and the chicken is caramelized on top, 13 to 14 minutes. Season with more salt to taste. Serve the chicken with the sauce and couscous or rice.

Red-Rubbed Grilled Chicken w/ Pom-Cauli Tabbouleh

SERVES 4 • ACTIVE TIME: 30 MINUTES **• TOTAL TIME:** 30 MINUTES

A boneless, skinless chicken breast is a terrible thing to waste, which can happen if you don't figure out a way to seal in moisture before cooking. Enter the spice paste, a great vehicle for transferring flavor to the meat while keeping it juicy. I purposely use dried garlic instead of fresh here; I like the way the powdery spices meld with olive oil and salt to perfectly coat the chicken. A quick cook and you're good to pair it with this low-carb tabbouleh. The pops of pomegranate, grassy herbs, toasty pine nuts, and crunchy cauliflower convey indulgent spa vibes.

¼ cup plus 2 tablespoons olive oil

1 tablespoon sweet paprika

1 teaspoon garlic powder

2 teaspoons kosher salt, plus more to taste

¼ teaspoon cayenne

4 thin-cut boneless, skinless chicken breasts (about 1¼ pounds)

⅓ cup pine nuts

½ medium cauliflower (1 pound)

4 cups lightly packed parsley leaves and tender stems

2 cups pomegranate seeds

1 tablespoon finely chopped jalapeño (seeded if desired)

⅓ cup freshly squeezed lemon juice (from 2 small lemons)

¼ teaspoon freshly ground black pepper, plus more to taste

1. Preheat the oven to 325°F. In a large bowl, combine ¼ cup of the olive oil, the paprika, garlic powder, 1 teaspoon of the salt, and the cayenne. Add the chicken, stir well to coat in the rub, and let rest on the counter (or in a Ziploc bag in the fridge for up to 24 hours) while you make the tabbouleh.

2. Arrange the pine nuts on a small rimmed baking sheet; toast until lightly golden, 6 to 7 minutes; remove from the oven to cool. By hand or using a food processor, finely chop the cauliflower (or pulse 5 times if using the processor) and transfer to a medium bowl, then finely chop the parsley (or pulse 25 times in the processor). Add to the bowl along with the pomegranate seeds, jalapeño, lemon juice, the remaining 2 tablespoons olive oil, remaining 1 teaspoon salt, and the pepper and toss to combine. Season with more salt and pepper.

3. Preheat a grill or grill pan over medium-high heat. Grill the chicken until grill marks form and the juices run clear when sliced, 2 to 3 minutes per side. Season with salt and pepper. Stir the pine nuts into the tabouleh, divide among four plates, and serve with the chicken.

**To make your own thin-cut chicken breasts, slice two 10-ounce boneless, skinless chicken breasts through the middle.*

Za'atar-Honey Chicken Wings w/ Spicy Tahini Dipping Sauce

SERVES 6 • ACTIVE TIME: 15 MINUTES **• TOTAL TIME:** 45 MINUTES

When you want chicken wings and nothing else will do, give these a spin. If you have time, marinate them for a few hours. It's not necessary, just an added bonus that will help the za'atar flavor really permeate the meat. Baking, versus the more conventional frying, simplifies the process but sacrifices nothing in texture or taste. A little brush of honey at the end along with a spicy dip, and you're game-day (or any day) ready.

- 2 lemons
- 3 pounds chicken wings, patted dry
- 1¾ teaspoons kosher salt, plus more to taste
- 3 tablespoons olive oil, plus more for brushing
- 6 tablespoons Za'atar Spice Blend (page 15 or store-bought)
- 1 tablespoon finely minced garlic
- 1½ teaspoons sweet paprika
- ½ teaspoon cayenne
- 3 tablespoons pure tahini paste
- 2 tablespoons water
- 1 tablespoon Harissa (page 15 or store-bought)
- 3 tablespoons honey

1. Preheat the oven to 425°F. Line a large rimmed baking sheet with parchment paper and arrange a rack on top. Lightly brush the rack with olive oil. Finely zest one of the lemons; reserve the zest. Juice both lemons (you should have about 6 tablespoons) into a large bowl. In a large bowl, toss the wings with the lemon zest, 3 tablespoons of the lemon juice, and 1½ teaspoons of the salt until the skin absorbs most of the juice, 30 seconds. Add the olive oil, 5 tablespoons of the za'atar, the garlic, paprika, and cayenne. Use a silicone spatula to stir until well coated. (If you have time, marinate on the counter for up to 2 hours or in the fridge for up to 24 hours.) Arrange the wings on the prepared rack, plump side down, with space between them. Bake until golden and slightly crisp, 20 minutes.

2. In a small bowl, combine the tahini, 2 tablespoons of the lemon juice, the water, harissa, and the remaining ¼ teaspoon salt; set aside.

3. Remove the baking sheet from the oven. Using tongs, flip the wings and return to the oven to bake until the tops of the wings are crisped, 10 minutes.

4. In a small bowl, combine the honey with the remaining 1 tablespoon za'atar and a generous pinch of salt (if needed, loosen with a little of the remaining 1 tablespoon lemon juice for easy brushing). Remove the wings from the oven, brush with the honey mixture, return to the oven, and bake until glazed and crispy, 6 to 7 more minutes. Serve with the dipping sauce.

Spice-Drawer Schnitzel w/ Pickle Mayo Sauce

SERVES 4 • ACTIVE TIME: 20 MINUTES **• TOTAL TIME:** 30 MINUTES

The three-step process of shuttling chicken cutlets between flour, egg, and breadcrumbs is something I've done thousands of times, so I thought I'd try cutting out a step and upping the impact by creating a flavorful batter and a seedy (in the good way) breading, enabling a double-dip instead of a triple. The pickle-studded mayo—a sort of poor-man's remoulade—is great for dipping or as a spread should you decide to stuff this winner inside a pita.

- 1¾ cups panko breadcrumbs
- ½ cup sesame seeds
- 1½ teaspoons whole cumin seeds
- 1 tablespoon whole coriander seeds
- 1 teaspoon kosher salt, plus more for seasoning
- 1 teaspoon coarsely ground black pepper, plus more for seasoning
- ⅔ cup all-purpose flour
- 1 teaspoon smoked or sweet paprika
- ½ cup water
- 1 large egg
- 1½ tablespoons grainy Dijon mustard
- 4 small boneless, skinless chicken breasts (1¾ to 2 pounds), lightly pounded
- ½ cup mayonnaise
- ¼ cup chopped cornichons, plus 1 tablespoon brine
- Vegetable oil, for frying
- Lemon wedges, for serving

1. On a small rimmed baking sheet (or 10-inch rimmed plate), combine the panko, sesame seeds, cumin and coriander seeds, and ½ teaspoon each of the salt and pepper. In another small rimmed baking sheet or wide, shallow dish, combine the flour, paprika, and the remaining ½ teaspoon each salt and pepper. Whisk in the water until a thick paste forms. Whisk in the egg and 1 tablespoon of the mustard.

2. Season the chicken generously with salt and pepper. Line a rimmed baking sheet with parchment paper. Dip each piece of chicken in the flour-egg mixture (using tongs to grab the tapered end of the chicken helps keep your hands clean), let the excess drip off, then press firmly into the breadcrumbs on both sides. Arrange on the prepared baking sheet as you finish and, if you have time, let rest 15 minutes before frying (this helps the crumbs adhere better but is not necessary).

3. In a small bowl, whisk together the mayo, remaining ½ tablespoon mustard, the cornichons, brine, and 2 generous pinches of pepper; set aside.

4. Heat ¼-inch oil in a heavy skillet over medium heat until a breadcrumb sizzles on contact. Working in batches, fry the schnitzels until golden brown and crisp, 2 to 3 minutes per side, adding more oil to the skillet as needed. Drain on paper towels, season with salt and pepper, and serve hot with the pickle mayo sauce and lemon wedges.

1

2

3

Sheet Pan Chermoula Chicken w/ Red Cabbage & Sweet Potatoes

SERVES 6 • ACTIVE TIME: 25 MINUTES • **TOTAL TIME:** 1 HOUR 30 MINUTES

As versatile as schug, as flavorful as chimichurri, as herbaceous as salsa verde, North African chermoula will now be a recurring star in your dinner rotation. This lemony, ginger-and-cumin-laced green sauce takes a tray of chicken and veggies to new heights. Starting with a spatchcocked chicken (back removed, bird flattened slightly) ensures faster, more even cooking. Spatchcock the chicken yourself, or ask your butcher to do it for you.

- 6 garlic cloves
- 2-inch piece fresh ginger, peeled and roughly chopped
- 2 lemons
- 2 cups lightly packed cilantro leaves and tender stems
- 1½ cups lightly packed parsley leaves and tender stems
- 2 teaspoons ground cumin
- 1½ teaspoons sweet paprika
- ½ teaspoon cayenne
- 3½ teaspoons kosher salt
- ⅔ cup olive oil
- 1 small red cabbage (1½ pounds), cut into ¼-inch-thick wedges
- 3 small or 2 medium sweet potatoes (1½ pounds), cut into ½-inch-thick wedges
- 1 large onion, cut into ¼-inch wedges
- 1 whole chicken (3½ to 4 pounds), spatchcocked (see page 18) and patted dry
- ¼ cup water

1. Preheat the oven to 400°F. In a food processor, process the garlic and ginger until finely minced, 10 to 15 seconds. Cut one lemon into wedges and reserve. Finely zest the other lemon directly into the processor. Juice the lemon; reserve the juice (you should have about 3 tablespoons). Add the cilantro, parsley, cumin, paprika, cayenne, and 1½ teaspoons of the salt to the processor; pulse until the herbs are finely processed, scraping down the sides as needed. Transfer to a medium bowl; stir in ⅓ cup of the olive oil and the reserved lemon juice. Transfer ½ cup chermoula to a small serving bowl; reserve.

2. Drizzle the remaining ⅓ cup olive oil over the bottom of a large baking sheet. Sprinkle the remaining 2 teaspoons salt evenly over the oil. Arrange the cabbage, sweet potatoes, and onions on the baking sheet in a single layer, then turn them over to coat both sides.

3. Pat the chicken dry. Arrange, breast side down, on top of the vegetables. Dollop ¼ cup of the chermoula on top, under the skin, and inside the cavity of the chicken; brush or rub with your hands to coat well. Flip the chicken breast side up; rub with an additional ¼ cup chermoula. Pour the water onto the baking sheet and tilt to distribute. (If you have time, marinate for 15 minutes.)

4. Roast until the vegetables are slightly charred in parts, the chicken legs jiggle, and the juices run clear, 55 minutes to 1 hour. Cut the chicken directly on top of the vegetables (I use kitchen shears); serve with the reserved chermoula and lemon wedges.

Deli Salad–Topped Grilled Chicken

SERVES 4 • ACTIVE TIME: 20 MINUTES • **TOTAL TIME:** 25 MINUTES

Give it up to Italian deli culture for inspiring so many of the delicious elements to this main-course salad, which also features grilled chicken and perfectly sharp arugula leaves. This one leans heavily on jars—marinated artichoke hearts, pickled pepperoncini, olives, and roasted peppers—to bring the most flavor with the least amount of work. Grill the chicken, toss with the arugula, and enjoy.

¾ cup (4 ounces) pitted olives of your choice, chopped

2 whole fire-roasted red peppers (5 ounces), drained and patted dry, chopped

1 cup drained, marinated artichoke hearts (from an 8-ounce jar), chopped*

3 ounces salami, diced (½ cup)

3 tablespoons drained, sliced pickled pepperoncini peppers

½ small red onion, thinly sliced

1 large lemon

3 tablespoons olive oil

Four 6-ounce boneless, skinless chicken breast cutlets

½ teaspoon kosher salt, plus more for seasoning

½ teaspoon freshly ground black pepper, plus more for seasoning

3 cups (2½ ounces) loosely packed arugula leaves

2 cups loosely packed basil leaves, chopped

1. In a medium salad bowl, combine the olives, roasted peppers, artichoke hearts, salami, pepperoncini, and onions. Thinly slice 4 rounds off the lemon and reserve, then juice the rest of the lemon (you should have about 2½ tablespoons) into the bowl; add 2 tablespoons of the olive oil.

2. Preheat a grill or grill pan over medium-high heat. Brush the chicken and lemon slices with the remaining 1 tablespoon olive oil and season generously with salt and pepper. Arrange the chicken and lemon slices on the grill; grill until the chicken is cooked and the lemons are slightly caramelized, 2 to 3 minutes per side. Transfer the chicken to a plate, season with more salt and pepper, and cover with foil to keep warm. Transfer the lemons to a cutting board, finely chop, and add to the salad bowl with the arugula, basil, and the ½ teaspoon each salt and pepper; gently toss. Divide the chicken and salad among four plates; season with more salt and pepper if desired.

**If you don't have marinated artichoke hearts, toss drained water-packed artichoke hearts with your favorite Italian salad dressing.*

Toum-ish Chicken Thighs w/ Roasted Radishes, Apples & Fennel

SERVES 6 • ACTIVE TIME: 20 MINUTES **• TOTAL TIME:** 1 HOUR

Think of Lebanese toum as the world's garlickiest and most delicious aïoli, made by blending an almost socially unacceptable amount of garlic with oil and salt into a fluffy, snow-white emulsion. I cheat by starting with mayonnaise, adding garlic to evoke toum's distinctive flavor profile. Brushing it on bone-in chicken thighs rested over a bed of vegetables before roasting creates a super-easy sheet pan dinner; expect to be swiping bites of the garlicky, schmaltzy veggies straight from the pan.

- 7 garlic cloves, finely grated on a Microplane or finely minced
- ⅓ cup mayonnaise (preferably olive oil mayo)
- 2 teaspoons kosher salt, plus more for seasoning
- 1 teaspoon sweet paprika
- 2 medium or 1 very large head fennel (1 pound), halved, cored, and thinly sliced, fronds reserved
- 3 large or 6 medium radishes, thinly sliced
- 1 medium red apple (such as Pink Lady), halved, cored, and thinly sliced
- ½ small red onion, thinly sliced
- ¼ teaspoon freshly ground black pepper, plus more for seasoning
- 2 tablespoons olive oil
- 8 medium or 6 large bone-in, skin-on chicken thighs (2¼ to 2½ pounds)
- Finely grated zest of 1 large lemon

1. Preheat the oven to 425°F. To make the toum, in a small bowl, combine the garlic, mayonnaise, 1 teaspoon of the salt, and the paprika. Transfer 3 or 4 tablespoons of the toum to a small bowl and reserve for serving.

2. On a large rimmed baking sheet, arrange the fennel, radishes, apples, and onions. Toss with the pepper, the remaining 1 teaspoon salt, and the olive oil. Nestle the chicken, skin side down, among the vegetables. Brush each piece with 1 teaspoon of the toum, flip, and brush the skin side of each piece with another 1 teaspoon toum, spreading some of it under the skin. Season the tops of the chicken with salt and pepper; roast until the vegetables are softened and browned in parts and the chicken is golden and the juices run clear, 40 to 45 minutes. Garnish with fennel fronds and the lemon zest. Serve the chicken with the vegetables and extra toum.

Simple Rotisserie-Style Chicken

SERVES 4 TO 6 • ACTIVE TIME: 5 MINUTES
TOTAL TIME: 1 HOUR 45 MINUTES

I wanted a basic, flavorful chicken reminiscent of store-bought rotisserie-type birds. Making one at home is cost-effective, and you have control over the chicken you buy and the seasonings you use. You can use this recipe wherever cooked chicken is called for (such as Hawaiij Chicken Salad, page 190). I saw my friend and talented home cook Sabrina Shance roast a chicken on parchment paper on her Instagram feed, and got hooked on the method. Not only do the chicken juices pool on the paper into flavorful drippings, but it makes for easy cleanup, too.

- 1½ tablespoons olive oil
- 2 teaspoons kosher salt, plus more for seasoning
- 1 teaspoon garlic powder
- 1 teaspoon onion powder
- 1 teaspoon sweet paprika
- 1 whole chicken (4 pounds), patted dry
- Freshly ground black pepper

1. Preheat the oven to 375°F. Line a 9 × 13-inch glass baking dish with parchment paper.

2. In a small bowl, combine the olive oil, salt, garlic powder, onion powder, and paprika.

3. Place the chicken, breast side up, in the prepared baking dish and season the cavity generously with salt and pepper. Use a pastry brush (or your hands) to coat the chicken all over with the spice blend.

4. Roast until the skin is golden, the legs jiggle, and the internal temperature reads 165°F at the thigh, 1 hour 20 minutes to 1 hour 30 minutes. Let rest for 10 minutes, gently remove and discard the parchment, then cut into pieces right in the pan and serve with the juices.

Shawarma-Spiced Turkey Pita Smashburgers

SERVES 4 • ACTIVE TIME: 30 MINUTES **• TOTAL TIME:** 30 MINUTES

Will you still be my friend if I confess that I'm not always a huge fan of the conventional burger? I prefer meat with some edge, and a patty can sometimes lack that good sear. Enter this smashburger, made with ground poultry seasoned with a pared-down, yet still punchy, shawarma spice. A hot skillet first caramelizes the meat and then toasts the pita side to a deep crunch, guaranteeing two separate but equally satisfying textural elements.

- 1 small onion
- 1½ teaspoons ground cumin*
- ¼ teaspoon ground turmeric*
- ¼ teaspoon ground cinnamon*
- 1 pound ground turkey (or chicken; preferably a combination of light and dark meat)
- ¼ cup finely chopped cilantro
- 2 garlic cloves, minced
- 1 teaspoon kosher salt, plus more for seasoning
- ¼ teaspoon freshly ground black pepper, plus more for seasoning
- Two 5- to 6-inch pitas, split into 4 total rounds
- 4 tablespoons olive oil
- Tahini Sauce (page 16) or well-stirred pure tahini paste, for serving
- Schug (page 17 or store-bought) and Amba (page 14 or store-bought), for serving

1. Grate the onion on the large holes of a box grater into a large bowl (you should have about ½ cup). Stir in the cumin, turmeric, and cinnamon, then mix in the turkey, cilantro, garlic, salt, and pepper with your hands or a silicone spatula until incorporated.

2. Arrange the pita rounds, insides up, on a clean work surface and spread one-quarter of the meat mixture out to the edge of each pita (the meat shrinks, so this is important). Season with salt and pepper.

3. Heat a large (12-inch) dry nonstick or cast-iron skillet over high heat. Add 2 tablespoons of the olive oil and arrange two of the pitas, meat side down, in the skillet and cook, pressing occasionally with a spatula, until the underside is deeply caramelized, 4 to 5 minutes. Flip and cook until the pitas are golden and crisp, 1 to 2 minutes. Wipe out the pan, add the remaining 2 tablespoons olive oil, and repeat with the remaining 2 pitas. Transfer to a cutting board, cut in halves or quarters, and drizzle with tahini. Serve with tahini sauce, schug, and amba.

**Cumin, turmeric, and cinnamon can be replaced with 2 teaspoons total store-bought shawarma spice blend.*

One-Pan Chicken Drumstick Tagine

SERVES 4 • ACTIVE TIME: 25 MINUTES **• TOTAL TIME:** 1 HOUR 15 MINUTES

Gorgeously golden, saucy, and satisfying, this one-skillet tagine (named for the Moroccan vessel it's traditionally made in) unifies its ingredients quickly in the pan to create a rich shortcut sauce that cloaks humble drumsticks, elevating them to something special. This type of tagine almost always includes dried fruit; I used apricots, but feel free to swap in some pitted prunes as well.

- 3 tablespoons olive oil
- 8 chicken drumsticks (about 2 pounds)
- ½ teaspoon kosher salt, plus more for seasoning
- ¼ teaspoon freshly ground black pepper, plus more to taste
- 1 jumbo onion, thinly sliced (about 3 cups)
- 3 garlic cloves, minced
- 1½-inch piece fresh ginger, peeled and finely minced (1½ tablespoons)
- 1 teaspoon ground cinnamon
- ½ teaspoon ground turmeric
- 2 cups water
- ⅔ cup finely chopped cilantro
- 12 dried apricots (5 ounces), halved
- 1 dried red chile, such as chile de arbol
- ½ small Preserved Lemon (page 17 or store-bought), seeded and chopped (¼ cup)*
- Cooked couscous, for serving

Heat the olive oil in a large (10- or 12-inch) skillet with a lid (which you'll use later) over medium heat. Season the chicken with the salt and pepper and brown, turning once or twice, until golden on all sides, 7 to 8 minutes. Transfer the chicken to a plate, then add the onions to the skillet with a pinch of salt and cook, stirring, until lightly golden, 8 to 9 minutes. Reduce the heat to medium-low, add the garlic, ginger, cinnamon, and turmeric, and cook, stirring, until fragrant, 2 minutes. Add the water along with half the cilantro, the apricots, dried chile, and preserved lemon. Nestle the chicken back into the skillet, bring to a boil, reduce the heat to a simmer, cover, and cook until the chicken is tender and the sauce has thickened, 40 minutes. Uncover, remove the dried chile, season with more salt and pepper if desired, and garnish with the remaining cilantro. Serve with couscous.

**Preserved lemon can be replaced with the juice and finely grated zest of 1 lemon plus 1 additional teaspoon kosher salt.*

Sheet Pan Shipudim (Skewers) w/ Za'atar Potato Wedges

SERVES 4 • ACTIVE TIME: 15 MINUTES • **TOTAL TIME:** 45 MINUTES

Pargiyot (boneless, skinless chicken thighs) are a natural for marinating, skewering, and grilling. They resist overcooking, staying juicy while the exteriors crisp up even without skin. They take on flavor really well, and they pair really nicely with all kinds of sides—in this case, couldn't-be-simpler za'atar-dusted potato wedges that roast away while the pargiyot roast. If you have the time and forethought, go ahead and marinate the chicken for a few hours.

- 1½ pounds (5 to 6) boneless, skinless chicken thighs (pargiyot)
- 3 tablespoons olive oil
- 2½ teaspoons ground cumin
- 2 teaspoons smoked paprika
- 2½ teaspoons kosher salt, plus more for seasoning
- 1 teaspoon silan (date syrup) or dark brown sugar
- ¼ teaspoon cayenne
- 3 large russet or Idaho potatoes (2 pounds), skin-on, scrubbed
- 3 tablespoons Za'atar Spice Blend (page 15 or store-bought)
- Freshly ground black pepper

1. Arrange two racks in the top and bottom thirds of the oven; preheat the oven to 425°F.

2. Cut each chicken thigh into 1½- to 2-inch-wide strips (you should have around 16 strips total). In a large bowl, whisk 2 tablespoons of the olive oil with the cumin, smoked paprika, 1½ teaspoons of the salt, silan, and cayenne. Add the chicken and toss to coat. Marinate on the counter while preparing the potatoes (or marinate in the fridge for up to 24 hours, removing 30 minutes before cooking).

3. Cut the potatoes into 6 or 8 wedges each and arrange them on a large rimmed baking sheet. Drizzle with the remaining 1 tablespoon olive oil. Sprinkle with the za'atar and remaining 1 teaspoon salt; stir to coat. Arrange in a single layer (as much as possible); roast on the lower rack until the potatoes are lightly browned and crisp around the edges, flipping once midway through, 30 to 35 minutes.

4. While the potatoes are roasting, fold each marinated chicken strip in half and thread 3 or 4 folded strips each onto four 8-inch skewers; arrange on a rimmed baking sheet.

5. During the last 15 minutes of the potatoes roasting, place the skewers on the top rack and roast until golden and browned around the edges (for darker chicken, broil an additional 2 to 3 minutes). Season the skewers with salt and pepper and serve with the potatoes.

Beef & Lamb

Yemenite-Spiced Steak w/ Mashed Potatoes & Greens

SERVES 4 • ACTIVE TIME: 25 MINUTES **• TOTAL TIME:** 45 MINUTES

So easy, so good! This steakhouse-worthy dinner incorporates classic Yemenite seasoning in new ways: hawaiij in the potatoes (not to mention swapping in olive oil for the more traditional butter), schug in the spinach—and lots of love in all of it.

- One 2-pound (1½-inch-thick) bone-in rib eye steak
- 1½ pounds (about 4) medium skin-on waxy potatoes, quartered
- 7 garlic cloves (3 left whole, 4 thinly sliced)
- 1 tablespoon plus 1 teaspoon kosher salt, plus more for seasoning
- ⅓ cup plus 1 tablespoon olive oil
- 1 tablespoon Hawaiij Spice Blend (page 16 or store-bought), plus more to taste
- 1 large bunch scallions
- Coarsely ground black pepper, for seasoning
- 1 pound (16 cups) boxed or bagged baby spinach
- 2 tablespoons Schug (page 17 or store-bought), plus more for serving

1. Remove the steak from the fridge to rest on the counter. Place the potatoes and the 3 whole garlic cloves in a medium lidded saucepan, cover with 2 inches of cold water, and add 1 tablespoon of the salt. Bring to a boil, reduce the heat to medium, and cook, partially covered, on a low boil until the potatoes are easily pierced with a fork, 25 to 30 minutes. Reserve 1½ cups of the cooking liquid, drain the potatoes, return them to the pot and, while hot, add ⅓ cup of the olive oil, ½ cup of the cooking liquid, the hawaiij, and the remaining 1 teaspoon salt. Mash until chunky-smooth, adding more liquid as needed. Cover to keep warm.

2. Preheat the oven to 500°F. Brush the scallions with the remaining 1 tablespoon olive oil and generously season the scallions and steak with salt and pepper. Heat a large (12-inch) dry cast-iron or other heavy ovenproof skillet over medium heat for 3 to 4 minutes. Add the steak and scallions and cook until caramelized and browned, 5 to 6 minutes per side. Remove the scallions to a plate, use an oven mitt to transfer the steak to the oven, and cook until the underside is deeply golden and caramelized, another 5 minutes for medium-rare or 7 to 8 for medium. Remove from the oven, transfer to a cutting board, and cover loosely with foil. With the heat off (the skillet should still be very hot), add the 4 sliced garlic cloves to the rendered fat in the skillet and cook, stirring, until softened and fragrant, 2 to 3 minutes. Working in batches, add the spinach to the skillet and cook, stirring, until wilted, 3 to 4 minutes. Stir in the schug and season with salt. Slice the steak across the grain. Serve the mashed potatoes with the spinach, steak, scallions, and additional schug, if desired.

Sloppy Yossi Sandwiches

SERVES 4 • ACTIVE TIME: 15 MINUTES **• TOTAL TIME:** 30 MINUTES

When I make this saucy sandwich it takes me back to the occasional night when my mom would open a can of Manwich sauce, mix it with ground beef, and call it dinner. This homemade version—my take on the classic—is renamed using the Hebrew nickname equivalent of "Joe" or "Joey." I add brown sugar to evoke the sweet notes in the original, but preserved lemons and harissa make the mix deep and complex. Since everything is stuffed into a pita, nothing escapes like it does when you use sliced bread, leaving you (and your white shirt) stainless.

- 3 tablespoons olive oil
- 1 pound lean (90/10) ground beef
- 1 medium onion, finely diced
- 1 medium green bell pepper, diced
- 3 tablespoons pitted, sliced green olives of your choice
- 3 garlic cloves, minced
- 1 teaspoon ground cumin
- One 15-ounce can tomato sauce
- ¼ cup water
- 2 tablespoons Harissa (page 15 or store-bought), plus more to taste
- 2 tablespoons dark brown sugar or silan (date syrup)
- 1½ teaspoons kosher salt, plus more for seasoning
- ½ cup chopped cilantro
- 2 tablespoons chopped Preserved Lemon (page 17 or store-bought), plus more to taste
- 4 pitas, tops removed, split
- Lettuce leaves, for serving

Heat 1 tablespoon of the olive oil in a large skillet over medium heat. Add the ground beef and cook, breaking up with a wooden spoon, until just cooked through and no longer pink, 4 to 5 minutes. Add the remaining 2 tablespoons olive oil, then add the onions, bell pepper, olives, garlic, and cumin and cook, stirring, until the vegetables soften, 5 to 6 minutes. Stir in the tomato sauce, water, harissa, brown sugar, and salt. Bring to a simmer, reduce the heat to low, cover, and simmer, stirring occasionally, until the meat is tender and the sauce has thickened, adding an extra splash of water if necessary, 15 minutes. Remove from the heat and stir in the cilantro and preserved lemon. Adjust the seasoning with more salt, harissa, and preserved lemon to taste. Stuff each pita with some lettuce leaves and 1 cup of the filling.

Baksh
(Bukharan Meat & Herb Pilaf)

SERVES 6 TO 8
ACTIVE TIME: 30 MINUTES • **TOTAL TIME:** 1 HOUR 15 MINUTES

My longtime manicurist, Angela Godratola, who comes from Bukhara in Uzbekistan, described this rice dish so lovingly I had to try it at home. Baksh fuses meat, huge handfuls of chopped herbs, and short-grain rice into a hearty dish. She graciously granted me permission to add chickpeas and dried cherries, nontraditional but worthy additions. Though typically served on Shabbat and holidays, baksh makes for a relatively hands-off one-pot weeknight dinner. (Pictured at right with Georgian-Style Salad, page 72.)

- 1½ cups short-grain or sushi rice
- ¼ cup olive oil
- 1 pound (80/20) ground beef
- 1 jumbo onion, chopped (3 cups)
- One 15-ounce can chickpeas, drained and rinsed
- 2¼ cups hot tap water, plus more as needed
- 2½ teaspoons kosher salt
- 2 large or 3 medium bunches cilantro (leaves and tender stems), finely chopped (2 cups)
- 1 large bunch dill, finely chopped (1 cup)
- ⅓ cup dried cherries
- ½ teaspoon freshly ground black pepper
- Georgian-Style Salad (page 72), for serving

1. Place the rice in a bowl and cover with 2 inches warm water; soak for 30 minutes. (Soak the rice while you do the rest of the prep.) Drain the rice and rinse with cold water until the water runs clear, 15 to 30 seconds; drain well.

2. Heat a large dry saucepan with a lid over medium-high heat. Add the olive oil, then add the meat and cook, breaking up any lumps with a wooden spoon, until no longer pink, 4 to 5 minutes. Add the onions and cook, stirring, until translucent, 7 to 8 more minutes. Add the rice and cook, stirring, 1 to 2 minutes. Stir in the chickpeas, hot water, and 1 teaspoon of the salt. Bring to a boil, reduce the heat to medium-low, and cook, uncovered, until most of the liquid evaporates, 6 to 7 minutes.

3. Reserve ½ cup each of the cilantro and dill. Stir the remaining herbs and dried cherries into the rice with the remaining 1½ teaspoons salt and the pepper, reduce the heat to very low, cover, and cook until the rice is translucent and plump, 35 to 40 minutes (the rice will be slightly sticky, not fluffy). Turn off the heat. Let the rice sit, covered, for 5 minutes. Uncover, stir in the reserved herbs, season with salt and pepper to taste, and serve with salad.

Grilled Hoisin-Harissa Lamb Chops & Plums w/ Herb Salad

SERVES 4 • ACTIVE TIME: 20 MINUTES • **TOTAL TIME:** 35 MINUTES

When I was growing up, our kosher meat was delivered once a month from Chicago; we picked it up from a local synagogue. "Shopping" for dinner often meant heading out to the extra freezer in the garage and removing the package we planned to cook on any particular night. Lamb chops were a special treat then, and they still are now. The simple hoisin-harissa glaze is the crowning glory here; brush on toward the end to prevent smoking. The herb salad can be served alongside or on top.

3 tablespoons hoisin sauce

2 tablespoons Harissa (page 15 or store-bought)

3 plums, halved

½ teaspoon kosher salt, plus more for seasoning

Freshly ground black pepper

1 tablespoon olive oil, plus more for brushing

8 to 10 baby lamb chops (2 to 2½ pounds)

1 tablespoon freshly squeezed lime juice

1 cup dill fronds

1 cup picked mint leaves

1 cup picked parsley or cilantro leaves

¼ cup thinly sliced red onion

1. In a small bowl, combine the hoisin and harissa. Heat a grill or grill pan over medium-high heat.

2. Season the plums on their cut sides with salt and pepper. Brush the hot grill pan with oil, then grill the plums, cut side down, until softened and grill marks are visible, 3 to 4 minutes; transfer to a large plate and loosely cover with foil. Season the lamb chops with salt and pepper and grill until light grill marks appear, 2 to 3 minutes per side for medium-rare. Brush the tops of the chops with half the hoisin-harissa mixture, flip, and grill the underside until the sauce caramelizes slightly, 30 seconds. While the underside is grilling, brush the tops with the rest of the mixture, flip, and grill for 30 more seconds. Transfer to the plate with the plums, lightly cover to keep warm, and let the chops rest for 5 minutes while you make the salad.

3. In a medium bowl, whisk together the lime juice, ½ teaspoon salt, and the olive oil. Add the herbs and onion and gently toss. Season the chops with more salt; serve with the plums and herb salad.

Matbucha-Style Meatballs

SERVES 6 • ACTIVE TIME: 25 MINUTES **• TOTAL TIME:** 1 HOUR

Moroccan matbucha, also known as *salade cuite* in French, is a classic for a reason: Silky peppers, rich tomato sauce, and a very generous amount of olive oil are simmered for hours to reduce the liquid and produce a concentrated dip/condiment. Here I "cheat" by starting with jarred marinara (a first for me); if you use a good one with no sugar added (I like Rao's, Tuscanini, and Lidia's brands), the results can be surprisingly impressive. Since we're in a zariz state of mind, the meatballs—guaranteed to be tender thanks to the addition of egg and grated potato—bypass an initial searing step. Instead, they get dropped straight into the sauce, where they simmer and become one with their delicious surroundings.

- ⅓ cup olive oil
- 2 large bell peppers (color of your choice), cut into ¼-inch dice
- One 3- to 4-inch jalapeño (seeded, if desired), minced
- 2 tablespoons sweet paprika
- 3 teaspoons ground cumin
- Two 24-ounce jars good-quality marinara sauce, or 6 cups homemade sauce
- 1 teaspoon kosher salt, plus more to taste
- 1 small onion
- One 8-ounce russet potato, peeled
- 1 pound (80/20) ground beef
- 1 large egg
- ¼ cup finely chopped cilantro, plus more for garnish
- 1 teaspoon baking soda
- P'titim Tahdig (page 210) or rice, for serving
- Lemon wedges, for serving

1. Heat the olive oil in a wide (12-inch), high-sided saucepan over medium-high heat. Add the bell peppers and cook, stirring, until softened, 10 minutes. Add all but 2 teaspoons of the jalapeño with the paprika and 2 teaspoons of the cumin and cook, stirring, until fragrant, 2 minutes. Stir in the tomato sauce, season with salt to taste, and bring to a brisk simmer. Reduce the heat to low and simmer, stirring occasionally, until the sauce has thickened, 10 minutes.

2. Grate the onion and potato on the large holes of a box grater into a large bowl and add the beef, egg, cilantro, baking soda, reserved 2 teaspoons jalapeño, and the remaining 1 teaspoon each cumin and salt. Gently mix with your hands until combined. Form into 15 or 16 meatballs, gently drop into the sauce, and simmer, covered, gently swirling the saucepan occasionally, until the meatballs are cooked through, 35 to 40 minutes. Uncover, garnish with cilantro, season with salt, and serve with p'titim tahdig or rice and lemon wedges.

Persian-Inspired Pull-Apart Beef

SERVES 8 TO 10
ACTIVE TIME: 20 MINUTES • **TOTAL TIME:** 4 HOURS 30 MINUTES

I borrowed the amazing flavors of a classic Persian herb stew called gorme sabzi that I love to eat at Salimi, a Persian-Jewish restaurant in the Florentine neighborhood of Tel Aviv. In this slow-braised roast, which cooks to a meltingly fork-tender texture in a few hours, funky dried Persian limes—known in Hebrew as *limon parsi* and in Arabic *as limon omani*—really enhance the dish's flavor. If you can't find them, you can use fresh limes and their zest. Loads of cilantro and spinach plus canned kidney beans fill out the rich sauce, which only gets better the next day.

- 3 tablespoons olive oil
- 2 large onions, sliced
- 2 tablespoons tomato paste
- 2 teaspoons ground turmeric
- 1¼ cups finely chopped cilantro (tender leaves and stems, from 1 large bunch)
- 10 cups (10 ounces) baby spinach leaves
- 3 cups water
- 3 tablespoons pomegranate molasses, plus more for finishing
- 10 pitted prunes
- 2 dried Persian limes*, slightly crushed with the heel of a knife
- 1 teaspoon dried mint (or 1 tablespoon finely chopped fresh)
- 2 teaspoons kosher salt, plus more to taste
- One 4½-pound (or two 2¼- to 2½-pound pieces) chuck or shoulder roast
- Two 15-ounce cans kidney beans, drained and rinsed

Arrange a rack in the bottom third of the oven; preheat to 300°F. Heat the oil in a large Dutch oven over medium-high heat. Add the onions and cook, stirring, until softened, 8 minutes. Add the tomato paste and turmeric and cook, stirring, 2 more minutes. Add the cilantro and spinach in batches and cook, stirring, until wilted, 2 minutes. Add the water, pomegranate molasses, prunes, dried limes, mint, and salt, bring to a boil, then add the beef, spoon some of the sauce over the top, cover the surface with parchment paper, and cover the pot. Transfer to the oven and cook until the meat is almost fork-tender, 3½ hours. Remove from the oven, uncover, stir in the beans, re-cover, return to the oven, and let the meat cook until fork-tender, 30 to 40 minutes. Let rest for 10 minutes and use two large forks to pull the beef into smaller pieces. Season with salt to taste and finish with a drizzle of pomegranate molasses, if desired.

**If you can't find Persian limes, swap in the juice and finely grated zest of 1 lime.*

Miso, Silan & Baharat Short Ribs

SERVES 6 TO 8
ACTIVE TIME: 20 MINUTES • **TOTAL TIME:** 4 HOURS 20 MINUTES

I've always started short-rib recipes by deeply browning the meat on all sides—and if the spirit moves you, by all means go for it. But broiling them right in the roasting pan saves time, and once you drain off the rendered fat, you simply pour the easily-thrown-together braising liquid over the top, add the alliums and aromatics, cover, and let the oven do the work. Baharat adds an almost Chinese five-spice-like accent, and the combination of miso and silan meld to add revelatory sweet and savory notes to the meltingly soft ribs.

- 4½ to 5 pounds English-cut (square-ish) bone-in short ribs
- Kosher salt and freshly ground black pepper
- ⅓ cup blond (shiro) miso
- ½ cup silan (date syrup) or honey
- 1 tablespoon unseasoned rice vinegar or apple cider vinegar
- 3 tablespoons Baharat Spice Blend (page 15 or store-bought)
- ½ teaspoon dried red pepper flakes
- ¾ cup water, plus more as needed
- 3 small onions, quartered
- 15 large garlic cloves
- Scallion greens, for serving

1. Arrange a rack 5 inches from the broiler and preheat the broiler. Pat the ribs dry and arrange them in a heavy 10 × 15-inch roasting pan or large Dutch oven (make sure the sides are higher than the ribs, and it's OK if the ribs are cozy in the pan). Season the ribs generously with salt and pepper; broil until sizzling and browned, 6 to 7 minutes. Remove from the oven, flip the ribs, return to the oven, and broil until the tops are sizzling and browned, 5 to 6 minutes. While the ribs are broiling, in a small bowl whisk together the miso, silan, vinegar, baharat, red pepper flakes, and water.

2. Remove the ribs from the oven, transfer briefly to a plate, and drain off and discard the fat. Reduce the oven temperature to 300°F. Return the ribs to the pan, nestle in the onions and garlic, pour the sauce over the ribs, and tip the pan to distribute the liquid. Cover with parchment paper and seal very tightly with foil. Roast until the ribs are tender and falling off the bone, 3 to 4 hours (check at 3 hours, and if the ribs aren't tender and the liquid has evaporated, add an additional ½ cup water before continuing to cook). Remove from the oven, transfer the ribs to a serving platter (discard the bones or save for broth), and cover with foil to keep warm. Skim off and discard as much fat as you can (there will be a good amount; if you like, refrigerate the ribs and sauce separately, then skim and discard the fat and rewarm the ribs and skimmed sauce). Mash the garlic into the sauce (there should be a generous 1¼ cups sauce). Pour the sauce over the ribs and garnish with scallion greens.

Vegetarian Mains

Cheesy, Spicy Gnocchi w/ Greens & Beans

SERVES 4 • ACTIVE TIME: 20 MINUTES **• TOTAL TIME:** 30 MINUTES

Inspired by a midnight snack I made for Chrissy Teigen when we were working together on one of her cookbooks, this recipe brings a full meal together in one colorful, cheesy skillet. The store-bought gnocchi gives this bake big main-course energy. The beans add protein, the greens contribute silky, earthy virtue, and the cheese makes it downright sinful.

- One 1-pound package store-bought gnocchi
- 4 tablespoons olive oil
- 1 large red onion, finely diced
- 10 cups (9 to 10 ounces) assorted baby or sliced greens (spinach, kale, Swiss chard leaves)
- 1 cup low-sodium vegetable broth
- 2 tablespoons Harissa (page 15 or store-bought)
- 1 tablespoon blond (shiro) miso (or low-sodium soy sauce)
- ½ teaspoon kosher salt
- One 15-ounce can cannellini beans, drained and rinsed
- 1 cup halved cherry tomatoes
- ½ cup (2 ounces) crumbled feta cheese
- 1½ cups (6 ounces) grated sharp Cheddar cheese

1. Arrange a rack in the top third of the oven; preheat to 400°F.

2. Cook the gnocchi according to the package directions. Drain well, then transfer to a bowl and toss with 1 tablespoon of the olive oil to prevent sticking.

3. Heat the remaining 3 tablespoons olive oil in a large (12-inch) ovenproof skillet over medium-high heat. Add the onions to the skillet and cook, stirring often, until they begin to soften, 6 to 7 minutes. Working in three batches, add the greens with 1 to 2 tablespoons broth each time, stirring, until they are wilted but not completely shrunken, 3 to 4 minutes total.

4. Stir in the harissa, miso, remaining broth (about ½ cup), and salt, then stir in the beans, tomatoes, and feta. Stir in the gnocchi. Remove from the heat, sprinkle with the Cheddar, and bake until the cheese is melted and bubbly, 10 minutes. Raise the oven to broil and broil until lightly golden, 2 to 3 minutes. Remove from the oven and divide among bowls.

Hachapuri Pizza

MAKES 2 PIZZAS • ACTIVE TIME: 15 MINUTES **• TOTAL TIME:** 1 HOUR

Georgia (the country, not the American state) is truly the land of a thousand hachapuris. Everywhere you sit down to eat you can order a delicious, cheese-filled bread boat (the cheese version is actually called hachapuri adjaruli), golden and bubbly, often with an oozy egg yolk in the center. Feta, mozzarella, and ricotta cheeses are combined to form the rich, creamy topping; I started with store-bought pizza dough to help you get this indulgent pizza on the table quicker than it takes for you to learn how to pronounce hachapuri (for the record, it's ha-tcha-POO-ree), but I also provide a homemade dough recipe if you're so inclined.

- 4 large eggs
- 1 cup (4 ounces) crumbled feta cheese
- 2 cups (8 ounces) grated mozzarella cheese
- ½ cup (4 ounces) ricotta cheese (preferably full-fat)
- 2 garlic cloves, finely minced
- ½ teaspoon kosher salt, plus more for seasoning
- ½ teaspoon freshly ground black pepper, plus more for seasoning
- 2 tablespoons cornmeal
- 1 pound store-bought or homemade pizza dough (recipe follows), thawed if frozen, divided into 2 equal-sized balls
- 2 tablespoons olive oil, plus more for drizzling
- 2 tablespoons unsalted butter, cut into small pieces (or olive oil)
- 2 tablespoons chopped dill fronds, for garnish

1. Arrange a rack and pizza stone in the center of the oven; preheat to 500°F or 525°F (if you don't have a pizza stone, you can also preheat an inverted large, clean cast-iron skillet for 25 to 30 minutes or a heavy baking sheet for 10 to 15 minutes). In a medium bowl, beat 2 of the eggs, then mix in the feta, mozzarella, ricotta, garlic, salt, and pepper until incorporated. Sprinkle 1 tablespoon of the cornmeal onto a 10- or 11-inch pizza pan, oil your hands, and press one ball of the dough into a 4-inch round. Drizzle about 1 tablespoon of the olive oil on the dough and use your hands to stretch it to the edges of the pan, leaving a slightly raised lip around the edges. Repeat with the remaining 1 tablespoon cornmeal, remaining dough ball, and remaining 1 tablespoon olive oil.

2. Spread half the cheese filling out to the border of each dough round, then hollow out a 2-inch well in the center. Transfer to the oven. Bake until the dough is crisp and browned and bubbly, 11 to 12 minutes. Separate the yolks from the whites of the remaining 2 eggs; keep them in separate small bowls (reserve the egg whites for another use).

3. Remove the pizza from the oven and immediately slip a yolk into the well you made in the center (return the pizza to the oven at this point for 1 minute if you like, but it's not necessary). Dot with half the butter and scatter with 1 tablespoon of the dill. Cut into pieces with a pizza cutter. Repeat with the second prepared pizza and remaining egg yolk, butter, and dill.

Pizza Dough

MAKES TWO 8-OUNCE DOUGHS • ACTIVE TIME: 10 MINUTES
TOTAL TIME: 45 MINUTES

Usually, I call for a homemade version of something with the store-bought as the backup, but in the spirit of zariz, I flipped the script. If you're in the mood, here's a great and, yes, simple pizza dough recipe.

¾ cup (180 grams/ml) warm water (lukewarm/bathwater level)

1 tablespoon (13 grams) sugar

1 packet (2¼ teaspoons/7 grams) active dry yeast

1 tablespoon (15 ml/14 grams) olive oil, plus more as needed

2¼ cups (295 grams) all-purpose flour, plus more as needed

1½ teaspoons (9 grams) kosher salt

1. In a large bowl, whisk together the warm water and sugar, then sprinkle the yeast over it and let rest for 5 minutes until fluffy and frothy. Add the olive oil, then the flour, and stir with a wooden spoon until a sticky but single piece of dough forms. Stir in the salt.

2. Lightly flour a clean work surface; scoop out the dough onto it. Knead the dough until smooth but not dry, pressing the dough with the heel of your hand and folding over, turning 90 degrees, and repeating, adding flour by the tablespoonful if it's too sticky to work with (you shouldn't need much), 4 to 5 minutes, Transfer the dough to a lightly oiled bowl, cover with plastic wrap, and let rest in a warm place until doubled in size, 30 to 35 minutes.

3. Uncover the dough and divide it into two pieces. Keep the second piece covered with plastic wrap while you work with the first. Proceed with the hachapuri pizza recipe.

**If you only want to make one pizza, you can halve the recipe. Or you can refrigerate half the filling and make one the next day. Wrap one of the doughs in plastic and defrost on the counter for 3 hours before using.*

Stretchy Polenta w/ Zucchini, Tomatoes & Mushrooms

SERVES 4 AS A MAIN COURSE, 6 AS A FIRST COURSE
ACTIVE TIME: 25 MINUTES • **TOTAL TIME:** 45 MINUTES

Polenta as a main course is a genius move. With very little work (and expense), you get a substantial, and adaptable, polenta for a host of great flavors. Cheese is a classic addition to the luscious polenta: Mozzarella adds stretch, while feta brings salt and the tiniest bit of funk. Get the summery vegetable tray roasting before you start on the polenta and the whole thing will be on the table in no time.

- 12 ounces cremini or white button mushrooms, trimmed and quartered
- 12 ounces (2½ cups) cherry tomatoes
- 12 ounces (2 medium) zucchini, cut into ¼-inch rounds
- 15 large garlic cloves
- 5 fresh thyme sprigs, plus more for garnish
- ¼ cup olive oil, plus more for drizzling
- 2 teaspoons kosher salt, plus more for seasoning
- ½ teaspoon freshly ground black pepper, plus more for seasoning
- 1½ cups whole milk
- 1½ cups water
- ¾ cup instant polenta*
- ¾ cup (3 ounces) shredded mozzarella cheese
- 1 cup (4 ounces) crumbled feta cheese, plus more for topping
- 3 tablespoons unsalted butter

1. Preheat the oven to 450°F. Arrange the mushrooms, tomatoes, zucchini, garlic, and thyme on a large rimmed baking sheet. Drizzle with the olive oil, sprinkle with 1 teaspoon of the salt and ¼ teaspoon of the pepper, and stir to coat well. Roast, stirring once midway through, until the mushrooms are browned, the tomatoes soften and slump, and the zucchini and garlic are soft and golden in parts, 20 to 25 minutes. Remove from the oven and discard the thyme sprigs.

2. Combine the milk, water, remaining 1 teaspoon salt, and remaining ¼ teaspoon pepper in a medium saucepan. Whisk in the polenta, bring the mixture to a boil over medium-high heat, and cook, stirring often, 3 to 4 minutes. Reduce the heat to low and cook, whisking often, until very thick and large bubbles form on the surface, another 2 minutes. Remove from the heat, stir in the mozzarella, ½ cup of the feta, and the butter, let sit for a minute, then stir again to incorporate. Divide the polenta among four bowls and top with the roasted vegetables. Top each bowl with 2 tablespoons of the remaining feta, some thyme, a generous drizzle of olive oil, and salt and pepper to taste.

**If you would like to use regular polenta, the proportions remain the same. Simply cook the polenta until it's creamy and soft, 20 to 25 minutes.*

Vegan Eggplant Schnitzel & Harissa Russian Dressing Slaw

SERVES 6 • ACTIVE TIME: 30 MINUTES • **TOTAL TIME:** 1 HOUR

Both the batter and dressing for this crispy, crunchy eggplant "steak" use silken tofu and tahini, which help bind the crumbs to the eggplant (look for a wider, rather than longer, eggplant). Baking the schnitzel doesn't sacrifice any crispiness, and I really enjoy how light the finished product is. Serve the recipe as is, or serve the schnitzels in a pita with the salad, tahini, and all the fixings.

- One 16-ounce package silken tofu, drained
- ¼ cup well-stirred tahini
- 3 tablespoons Harissa (page 15 or store-bought)
- 1 tablespoon tomato paste
- ¾ cup olive oil
- 1½ tablespoons sugar
- 3 tablespoons apple cider vinegar
- 2¼ teaspoons kosher salt, plus more for seasoning
- ¼ cup finely chopped sweet pickles
- 1 medium eggplant (1¼ pounds)
- 2½ cups panko breadcrumbs
- Freshly ground black pepper, for seasoning
- ½ medium cabbage (green, red, or both, 1½ pounds), shredded (10 cups)
- ½ cup thinly sliced scallion greens

1. Preheat the oven to 450°F. In a blender, combine the tofu, tahini, harissa, tomato paste, 2 tablespoons of the olive oil, the sugar, 1 tablespoon of the vinegar, and 1½ teaspoons of the salt and blend on medium speed until smooth, 20 to 25 seconds. Transfer 1 cup of the mixture to a large bowl; stir in the pickles and the remaining 2 tablespoons vinegar; set aside for the slaw, but first reserve 6 tablespoons for serving in a small bowl.

2. Use a sharp knife to cut the eggplant lengthwise into six ½-inch-thick steaks (peel the skin off the end pieces). Arrange on a clean kitchen towel, season both sides with the remaining ¾ teaspoon salt, and let sit for 10 minutes. Pat dry on both sides.

3. Combine ½ cup of the olive oil and the panko in a 9 × 13-inch baking dish. Brush a large rimmed baking sheet with the remaining 2 tablespoons olive oil. Brush one cut side of an eggplant slice with 1½ tablespoons of the tofu coating. Press into the panko mixture, then repeat on the other side with another 1½ tablespoons of the dressing, then panko. Repeat with the remaining eggplant slices and panko, arranging on the prepared baking sheet as you go. Bake, flipping halfway through, until golden brown and crisp, 20 to 25 minutes total. Season with salt and pepper to taste. While the schnitzel is baking, add the cabbage and scallion greens to the bowl with the dressing reserved for the slaw; toss to coat. Serve the schnitzels with the slaw and remaining reserved dressing.

Golden Chickpea Soupy Stew

SERVES 6 • ACTIVE TIME: 25 MINUTES **• TOTAL TIME:** 50 MINUTES

Wintery, filling, and vegan, this stew-soup hybrid is inspired by the Yemenite versions I often eat at one of several neighborhood marakiyot (soup joints). It comes together in a snap but is special in its finished form. Hawaiij, a favorite bang-for-your-buck spice blend, definitely illuminates every bowl. Serving over rice turns this dish into a meal. Of course, you could use any canned beans you like in place of the chickpeas.

- 3 tablespoons olive oil
- 1 large onion, diced
- 1 red bell pepper, diced
- 1 tablespoon kosher salt, plus more for seasoning
- 3 large garlic cloves, minced
- 6 cups low-sodium vegetable broth, plus more for a brothier stew
- 1 medium potato (any kind will do!), peeled and diced
- 2 small carrots, diced
- Two 15-ounce cans chickpeas, drained and rinsed
- 2 tablespoons Hawaiij Spice Blend (page 16 or store-bought)
- Schug (page 17 or store-bought), lemon wedges, and pita or flatbread, for serving

Heat the oil in a large pot over medium-high heat. Add the onions and bell pepper with a pinch of salt and cook, stirring occasionally, until the onions are translucent and the pepper has softened, 7 minutes. Add the garlic and cook, stirring, until fragrant, 2 minutes. Add the broth, potatoes, carrots, chickpeas, hawaiij, and the salt and bring the stew to a boil. Reduce the heat to low and simmer until the potatoes are soft, the chickpeas have absorbed some of the liquid, and the stew has thickened slightly, 35 minutes. Use the back of the ladle or a potato masher to mash some of the stew to thicken slightly; add more broth if desired. Serve with schug, lemon wedges, and pita.

Roasted Cauliflower w/ Creamy Cashew Red Pepper Sauce

SERVES 4 • ACTIVE TIME: 20 MINUTES **• TOTAL TIME:** 1 HOUR 20 MINUTES

Cauliflower is the new steak: Discuss! With time spent hanging out in the oven, cauliflower turns simultaneously sweet, soft, and crisp. Like meat, this large cut of veg takes on flavor well and begs for interesting ingredient collaborations. I added some onions and garlic to the cauli roasting tray and used them in a shortcut creamy roasted red pepper sauce that incorporates cashews for extra creaminess.

- 1¾ teaspoons kosher salt, plus more for salting the water and for seasoning
- ⅓ cup raw cashews
- 1 large cauliflower (2½ pounds)
- ½ cup olive oil
- 2 teaspoons honey
- 1 teaspoon Dijon mustard
- 1 teaspoon chopped thyme leaves
- 1 teaspoon ground coriander or cumin
- ½ teaspoon ground turmeric
- 2 medium onions, halved through the root
- 5 large garlic cloves
- One 12-ounce jar fire-roasted red peppers, well drained and rinsed
- 1 tablespoon fresh lemon juice
- ¼ teaspoon cayenne, or more to taste

1. Fill a large pot a bit more than halfway with generously salted water. Bring to a boil over high heat. Place the cashews in a small heatproof bowl; use a ladle to remove 1 cup of the boiling water the pot and pour over the cashews. Soak until soft, 30 minutes; drain.

2. While the cashews soak, set the cauliflower, core side up, on a cutting board; cut into four quarters through the core. In a small bowl, combine 6 tablespoons of the olive oil, the honey, mustard, thyme, coriander, turmeric, and 1 teaspoon of the salt. Gently lower the cauliflower and onion halves into the boiling water, return to a boil, and cook, partially covered, until they begin to soften, 7 to 8 minutes. Lift out with a slotted spoon or spider, letting the excess water drip off. Transfer to a large rimmed baking sheet; cool slightly. Add the garlic to the baking sheet and brush everything with the spiced oil mixture. Roast until the cauliflower and onions are deeply golden in parts and the garlic is tender, 20 to 25 minutes.

3. Transfer the onions and garlic to a blender with the soaked cashews, roasted peppers, lemon juice, remaining 2 tablespoons olive oil, ¾ teaspoon salt, and the cayenne. Blend on high speed until creamy, 30 to 45 seconds. Season with more salt to taste. Spread the red pepper cream sauce on a serving plate and top with the cauliflower.

Lacquered Tofu & Warm Cabbage Bowls

SERVES 4 • ACTIVE TIME: 20 MINUTES **• TOTAL TIME:** 50 MINUTES

The strips of tofu starring in this recipe are definitely *not* trying to be chicken; they're reveling in their tofu-ness. When lavished with their glossy glaze, they roast up shiny, with deeply caramelized edges and tender centers. A dollop of creamy tahini sauce pulls the cabbage and tofu together perfectly. The cabbage looks like a lot on the roasting pan, but I promise it shrinks down to just the right amount.

- One 1-pound package firm or extra-firm tofu, drained
- 1 medium cabbage (2 pounds), cored and sliced into ½-inch-thick ribbons (12 packed cups)
- ¼ cup olive oil
- 2 teaspoons kosher salt
- ¾ teaspoon freshly ground black pepper
- ¼ cup pomegranate molasses, plus more for drizzling
- ¼ cup honey
- 2 tablespoons Harissa (page 15 or store-bought)
- 1½ teaspoons cornstarch
- 1 small red onion, halved and sliced
- Juice of 1 lemon (3 tablespoons)
- 1 tablespoon ground sumac
- 1 large carrot, shredded
- ½ cup picked cilantro leaves, plus more for garnish
- 1 medium avocado, sliced
- Tahini Sauce (page 16)

1. Arrange two racks in the top and bottom thirds of the oven; preheat to 400°F. Line a large rimmed baking sheet with parchment paper.

2. Cut the tofu lengthwise into ¼-inch-thick planks, stack the planks, and halve into rectangles. Arrange between two clean kitchen towels. Pat dry, applying pressure to remove moisture. Arrange the cabbage on another large rimmed baking sheet. Drizzle with the olive oil. Sprinkle with 1 teaspoon of the salt and the pepper; stir to coat well.

3. In a small bowl, whisk the pomegranate molasses, honey, harissa, cornstarch, and ½ teaspoon of the salt. Arrange the tofu on the prepared baking sheet. Brush ½ teaspoon of the glaze on each side of the tofu. Place the tofu on the top rack and the cabbage on the lower rack; roast for 10 minutes. Remove the tofu and cabbage from the oven. Brush the top of each piece of tofu with ½ teaspoon of the glaze, flip, and brush each piece with another ½ teaspoon. Stir the cabbage, return both sheets to the oven, and roast until the tofu is shiny and slightly caramelized and the cabbage is wilted and charred in spots, 13 to 15 minutes.

4. In a small bowl, toss the onion and lemon juice with the sumac and remaining ½ teaspoon salt; pickle on the counter, tossing occasionally.

5. In a large bowl, toss the cabbage with the carrots and cilantro.

6. Divide the cabbage mixture, tofu, pickled onions, and avocado among four bowls. Dollop some tahini sauce on top of each bowl and drizzle with pomegranate molasses.

Roasted Veg & Halloumi Crouton Salad

Grilled Basil Chicken & Nectarine Salad

Tunisian-ish Chickpea & Tuna Salad

Wedge Salad w/ Creamy Feta Dressing & Smoky Shiitakes

Mujadara Salad w/ Tahini Yogurt

Grilled Skirt Steak Pita Panzanella Salad

Hawaiij Chicken Salad

Herb & Cherry Salad–Topped Cheese Toasts

Main Course Salads

Roasted Veg & Halloumi Crouton Salad

SERVES 4 • ACTIVE TIME: 15 MINUTES **• TOTAL TIME:** 45 MINUTES

If you've been to Cyprus, Greece, Turkey, or Israel, pretty much every beachside restaurant has a Halloumi salad on the menu. Rubbery and firm, it's a cheese that, unlike most, actually takes on heat well. Frying or grilling are the typical cooking methods, but I found that a sheet pan (where you also roast the vegetables) makes easy work of developing a golden, crisp exterior while preserving the desired chewy interior. Splash on the red wine vinegar dressing to pretend like you're on the beach in Tel Aviv (flip-flops optional).

- 1 large zucchini (12 ounces), cut into 1-inch chunks
- 1 large red bell pepper, cut into 1-inch chunks
- One 10-ounce package Halloumi cheese, cut into 1-inch cubes
- 7 tablespoons olive oil
- 2 teaspoons dried oregano
- ¾ teaspoon kosher salt
- ½ teaspoon freshly ground black pepper, plus more for seasoning
- ¼ cup red wine vinegar
- 2 teaspoons Dijon mustard
- 1 teaspoon honey
- 5 cups chopped romaine lettuce (from 2 small or 1 large romaine heart)
- 2 medium vine-ripened tomatoes, cut into 1-inch chunks
- ½ small red onion, sliced
- ¼ cup kalamata olives, halved

1. Preheat the oven to 425°F. Line a rimmed baking sheet with parchment paper. In a large bowl, combine the zucchini, bell pepper, Halloumi, 3 tablespoons of the olive oil, 1 teaspoon of the oregano, ½ teaspoon of the salt, and ¼ teaspoon of the pepper and toss to coat. Transfer to the prepared baking sheet, evenly distributing to leave space between the vegetables and cheese. Roast until the cheese is golden and the vegetables are softened, 20 to 25 minutes. Cool for 10 minutes.

2. While the vegetables are cooling, in a jar with a tight-fitting lid (or a bowl), combine the remaining 4 tablespoons olive oil, remaining 1 teaspoon oregano, and remaining ¼ teaspoon each salt and pepper with the vinegar, mustard, and honey. Seal and shake (or whisk in the bowl) until creamy.

3. In a large salad bowl, combine the lettuce, tomatoes, and onions and toss with half the dressing. Top with the Halloumi, roasted vegetables, and olives, then drizzle with the remaining dressing and season with lots of pepper to taste.

Grilled Basil Chicken & Nectarine Salad

SERVES 4 • ACTIVE TIME: 20 MINUTES
TOTAL TIME (INCLUDING COOLING TIME): 35 MINUTES

Every cook needs a salad like this in their repertoire, one where a single star ingredient—in this case almost-instant pickled onions—ratchets everything up a few notches. Avocadoes and nectarines are a favorite pairing, as is the combination of stone fruit and basil, so think of this salad as a Venn diagram of goodness.

- 1 small red onion, sliced
- 2 large lemons, 1 finely zested, both juiced (1 tablespoon zest, ½ cup juice)
- 1 tablespoon ground sumac
- 1½ teaspoons kosher salt, plus more for seasoning
- 1 cup walnut halves (or pecans)
- 2 cups lightly packed basil leaves
- 5 tablespoons olive oil
- 1½ tablespoons Dijon mustard
- 2 teaspoons honey
- ½ teaspoon freshly ground black pepper, plus more for seasoning
- 1½ pounds (4 to 5) thin-cut boneless, skinless chicken breasts
- 6 cups butter lettuce leaves (from 2 small heads)
- 2 medium nectarines (or peaches), cut into wedges
- 1 firm but ripe avocado, sliced

1. Preheat the oven to 350°F. In a large salad bowl, toss the onions and 3 tablespoons of the lemon juice with the sumac and ½ teaspoon of the salt; toss occasionally while you prep the other ingredients until softened and pink.

2. Arrange the walnuts on a small baking sheet and sprinkle with salt. Roast until lightly fragrant, 6 to 7 minutes; cool and coarsely chop. Finely chop 1 cup of the basil; reserve the remaining as whole leaves.

3. In a large jar with a tight-fitting lid, combine the remaining 5 tablespoons lemon juice with the zest, the olive oil, mustard, honey, the remaining 1 teaspoon salt, and the pepper. Shake until creamy.

4. Pour ¼ cup of the dressing into a bowl or Ziplock bag, add the chopped basil and chicken, and toss to coat. Marinate on the counter while the grill heats (or in the fridge for up to 8 hours).

5. Heat a large grill or grill pan over medium-high heat, season the chicken with salt and pepper, and cook the chicken until grill marks appear, 2 to 3 minutes per side. Transfer to a cutting board, cool slightly, then slice.

6. Add the lettuce, nectarines, avocado, whole basil leaves, and chicken to the bowl with the onions. Add the remaining dressing and gently toss to coat. Top with the walnuts and season with salt and pepper to taste.

Tunisian-ish Chickpea & Tuna Salad

SERVES 4 • ACTIVE TIME: 15 MINUTES
TOTAL TIME (INCLUDING MINIMUM MARINATING TIME): 45 MINUTES

To paraphrase Shakespeare, Niçoise by any other name would taste as great. I took my inspiration from the classic French salad, marinating canned chickpeas for extra oomph. Good oil-packed jarred tuna and oil-cured Moroccan-style olives really enhance the proceedings, but pantry-staple canned tuna and kalamatas would also be great. Pro tip: If you like, pile the ingredients into toasted baguettes for a slapdash rendition of a Tunisian sandwich.

- 4 large eggs
- ¼ cup good-quality olive oil
- 2 lemons, 1 zested and juiced, 1 cut into wedges for serving
- 1 teaspoon Harissa (page 15 or store-bought)
- ½ teaspoon dried mint
- ¾ teaspoon kosher salt, plus more for seasoning
- One 15-ounce can chickpeas, drained and rinsed
- ½ cup chopped celery, plus any tender inner leaves for garnish
- ¼ cup thinly sliced red onion
- ½ cup chopped cilantro
- 1 small head butter lettuce, leaves separated (3 cups)
- One 7.7-ounce jar good-quality tuna in olive oil (such as Ortiz), drained, oil reserved
- ⅓ cup oil-cured black olives, pitted and halved
- Freshly cracked black pepper

1. In a medium bowl, combine 2 cups each ice and water. Place the eggs in a medium saucepan, cover with 2 inches water, season generously with salt (this actually seasons the eggs!), and bring to a boil. Reduce the heat to medium-low and simmer for 9 minutes. Use a slotted spoon to transfer the eggs to the ice bath, cracking them slightly so water permeates the shell. After 5 minutes, peel under cold running water, pat dry, and halve.

2. In a medium bowl, whisk together the olive oil, lemon zest and juice, harissa, mint, and salt. Add the chickpeas, celery, and onions and let sit for 30 minutes (or up to 2 hours) on the counter, or up to 24 hours in the refrigerator. Stir in the cilantro. Arrange the lettuce on a platter, spoon the chickpeas and their liquid over the lettuce, and top with the tuna, olives, and eggs. If desired, drizzle some of the reserved tuna oil over the salad, then season with salt and pepper to taste, garnish with celery leaves (if using), and squeeze some lemon wedges over the top.

Wedge Salad w/ Creamy Feta Dressing & Smoky Shiitakes

SERVES 4 TO 6 • ACTIVE TIME: 20 MINUTES **• TOTAL TIME:** 35 MINUTES

I can't think of anything more retro-American than a classic wedge salad, but here I've refitted it for my type of cooking using the ingredients I love. The dressing swaps in feta and labaneh for the usual blue cheese and sour cream, and toasted panko replaces croutons. The crowning glory is tiny, smoky-sweet bits of skillet shiitake "bacon" you'll have to guard closely, lest anyone in their midst snack on them until they're all gone.

- ½ cup mayonnaise
- ½ cup labaneh or Greek yogurt
- 3 tablespoons freshly squeezed lemon juice (from one lemon)
- ½ teaspoon freshly cracked black pepper, plus more to taste
- ¾ teaspoon kosher salt
- ¾ cup (3 ounces) crumbled feta cheese
- 5 tablespoons olive oil
- 1 teaspoon smoked paprika
- 2 teaspoons maple syrup
- 4 ounces shiitake mushroom caps, sliced
- ½ cup panko breadcrumbs
- 4 small heads Little Gem lettuce, halved (or 2 medium romaine hearts, quartered lengthwise)
- ¾ cup cherry tomatoes, halved
- ¼ cup chopped chives

1. In a small bowl, combine the mayonnaise, labaneh, lemon juice, pepper, and ¼ teaspoon of the salt. Stir in ½ cup of the feta; chill until ready to use. In another bowl, whisk 3 tablespoons of the olive oil with the smoked paprika, maple syrup, and ¼ teaspoon of the salt. Add the mushrooms and toss for 10 to 15 seconds to coat well. Heat a large dry nonstick or cast-iron skillet over medium heat.

2. Add the mushrooms, spread out in a single layer (as much as possible), and cook until the underside is crisp, 4 to 5 minutes. Stir (or flip individually if you have patience) and cook for an additional 2 minutes. Transfer to one-half of a dinner plate. Add the remaining 2 tablespoons olive oil to the skillet, then add the panko and remaining ¼ teaspoon salt and cook, stirring, until golden and crisp, 4 to 5 minutes. Transfer to the other half of the dinner plate. Arrange the lettuce halves on a platter. Thin the dressing with a little bit of water if needed and drizzle each half with 3 or 4 tablespoons of the dressing. Divide the tomatoes, shiitakes, breadcrumbs, and remaining ¼ cup feta among the halves, garnish with the chives, and top with pepper.

Mujadara Salad w/ Tahini Yogurt

SERVES 4 TO 6 • ACTIVE TIME: 15 MINUTES **• TOTAL TIME:** 40 MINUTES

Hello, hearty lentils and rice! Meet cool, crunchy lettuce and tomatoes, creamy tahini-infused yogurt, and a simple drizzle of lemon juice and olive oil in this salad inspired by mujadara, which has roots in Iraq and Lebanon. Oh, and don't forget to invite the oven-roasted caramelized onions, made with my hands-off sheet pan method. It'll spoil you for making this type of onions any other way. With this one, the last bite might be the best, after the salad's juices are on a first-name basis with the nutty yogurt and warm-spiced rice.

- ⅔ cup long-grain white rice*
- ½ cup dried green lentils, picked over*
- 2¼ cups water
- 2 medium onions, thinly sliced
- 10 tablespoons olive oil
- 1½ teaspoons ground cumin
- ½ teaspoon ground cinnamon
- 1½ teaspoons kosher salt, plus more for seasoning
- ½ cup chopped cilantro
- Finely grated zest and juice of 2 small lemons (3 teaspoons zest, 6 tablespoons juice)
- ¼ teaspoon freshly ground black pepper, plus more for seasoning
- ¾ cup plain yogurt
- ¼ cup well-stirred tahini
- 4 cups shredded crisp, green lettuce
- 1 pound assorted tomatoes, cut into 1-inch chunks

**You can start with 2 cups cooked rice and 1 cup drained, canned lentils if you have them.*

1. Preheat the oven to 425°F. Combine the rice and lentils in a strainer and rinse for 15 seconds. Transfer to a large pot, add the water, bring to a boil, reduce the heat to a simmer, cover, and cook until the rice and lentils are tender, 18 to 20 minutes. Uncover, fluff, and let cool to room temperature (you can speed up this process by spreading them out across a large rimmed baking sheet).

2. While the lentils and rice are cooking, arrange the onions on a large rimmed baking sheet, drizzle with 6 tablespoons of the olive oil, sprinkle with the cumin, cinnamon, and ½ teaspoon of the salt, toss to coat, and transfer to the oven. Roast, stirring once or twice, until some of the onions are quite blackened and the rest are caramelized and softened, 20 to 25 minutes.

3. Reserve ½ cup of the onions and transfer the rest along with the oil from the roasting pan into a medium bowl and add the rice, lentils, cilantro, 2 teaspoons of the zest, ½ teaspoon of the salt, and the pepper.

4. In a small bowl, combine the yogurt with the tahini, 3 tablespoons of the lemon juice, 1 tablespoon of the olive oil, the remaining 1 teaspoon of the zest, and ½ teaspoon salt.

5. Spread the yogurt-tahini mixture on the bottom of a large, lipped platter, then top with the lettuce, followed by the mujadara. Add the tomatoes to the bowl the mujadara was in and toss with the remaining 3 tablespoons each lemon juice and olive oil. Season with salt and pepper, pour over the mujadara, and top with the reserved onions.

Grilled Skirt Steak Pita Panzanella Salad

SERVES 4 TO 6 • ACTIVE TIME: 7 MINUTES **• TOTAL TIME:** 15 MINUTES

In this fattoush-panzanella mash-up, pita takes the place of the standard cubed bread you often see in these types of salads. Simply grilled steak and a punchy, capery dressing give this one Mediterranean cred. You can make the dressing and toast the pitas in advance, then grill the steak and assemble everything à la minute.

- Three 5- to 6-inch pitas (day-old is good!), each cut into 6 or 8 triangles
- ⅓ cup plus 2 tablespoons olive oil, plus more for the pan
- Kosher salt and freshly ground black pepper
- 1¼ pounds skirt steak, cut into two pieces
- 4 tablespoons capers, drained
- 3 tablespoons red wine vinegar
- 2 tablespoons silan (date syrup) or honey
- 2 tablespoons grainy Dijon mustard
- 5 cups (5 ounces) arugula leaves
- 1 pound assorted tomatoes, chopped
- ½ red onion, thinly sliced
- 1 small jalapeño (seeded if desired), cut into thin rings

1. Preheat the oven to 400°F. Arrange the pitas on a rimmed baking sheet, drizzle with 2 tablespoons of the olive oil, season with salt and pepper, and bake until toasted and crisp, 9 to 10 minutes.

2. Heat a large cast-iron skillet, grill pan, or grill over high heat. Pat the steaks dry and season generously with salt and pepper. Brush the grill or pan lightly with oil and cook the steaks until medium-rare, 4 to 5 minutes per side. Transfer to a cutting board to rest for 5 minutes, then slice against the grain into thin slices.*

3. Finely chop 3 tablespoons of the capers and add to a small bowl. Add the vinegar, silan, and mustard, then whisk in the remaining ⅓ cup olive oil in a steady stream until creamy. Season the dressing with salt and pepper to taste. Just before serving, in a salad bowl, toss the arugula, tomatoes, onions, jalapeño, and remaining 1 tablespoon capers, drizzle with the dressing, top with the steak and pitas, and gently toss again.

**To slice against the grain: Cut the steak along the grain (lines) into 3-inch pieces, then rotate the pieces 90 degrees and slice the steak into thin slices; the interior of the steak should look like a mosaic of tiny squares.*

Hawaiij Chicken Salad

MAKES 4 CUPS • ACTIVE TIME: 20 MINUTES
TOTAL TIME (INCLUDING COOLING TIME): 25 MINUTES

Think curry chicken salad, but with a twist. The crunchy celery and almonds, juicy grapes, and creamy mayo turn "lunch staple" into "lunch special." Though simple sandwich bread also does the trick, lettuce spears are my preferred vehicle here. Hawaiij and curry powder bear many similarities, so if you don't have one, use the other. You can use the meat from my Simple Rotisserie-Style Chicken (page 134) or any cooked chicken you have; both light and dark meat work really well here.

- ½ cup raw almonds
- ½ cup mayonnaise
- Finely grated zest and juice of 1 small lemon (2 teaspoons zest, 3 tablespoons juice)
- 1 tablespoon Dijon mustard
- 2 teaspoons Hawaiij Spice Blend (page 16 or store-bought), or more to taste, or curry powder
- 1 teaspoon kosher salt
- ¼ teaspoon freshly ground black pepper, plus more to taste
- 1 pound cooked store-bought rotisserie chicken meat (white, dark, or a combination, or from 1 recipe Simple Rotisserie-Style Chicken, page 134), chopped (2½ cups)
- ½ cup finely diced celery
- ½ cup thinly sliced red grapes
- ⅓ cup finely diced red onion
- 1 tablespoon finely diced jalapeño
- Lettuce leaves and/or sandwich bread, for serving

Preheat the oven to 350°F. Arrange the almonds on a small rimmed baking sheet; toast until fragrant and golden, 10 minutes. Cool and coarsely chop. In a medium bowl, whisk together the mayonnaise, lemon zest and juice, mustard, hawaiij, salt, and pepper until smooth. Gently fold in the chicken, toasted almonds, celery, grapes, onions, and jalapeño until coated in the dressing. Season with pepper to taste. Serve on lettuce leaves, or as a sandwich on bread with lettuce.

Herb & Cherry Salad–Topped Cheese Toasts

SERVES 2 • ACTIVE TIME: 20 MINUTES • **TOTAL TIME:** 20 MINUTES

Every summer at HaBasta, a favorite restaurant of mine just off the shuk, the "Lali" salad—ripe market cherries tossed with raw minced garlic, cilantro leaves, and a vinegary dressing—appears on the menu for a few short weeks. The person behind the dish is chef and writer Hila Alpert, whose nickname, Lali, inspired the salad's moniker. Alpert was raised in the Judean Hills on Kibbutz Ma'Aleh HaHamisha, one of the first places in Israel to successfully grow cherries as a crop. "So I basically grew up with cherries in my hands," said Alpert, a legend on the Israeli food scene who's known as having *hayad*, or "the hand"—meaning born-with-it talented. Alpert recommends making the salad only when cherries are at their peak, so I make this toast—whose mild cheese supports, rather than competes with, the salad's distinct flavor mix—only when the time is just right.

- 1½ cups (8 ounces) fresh cherries, pitted and halved
- 1 small shallot, thinly sliced (¼ cup)
- 1½ tablespoons olive oil, plus more for brushing the bread
- 1½ tablespoons balsamic vinegar
- Two 1½-inch-thick slices crusty bread
- 6 ounces creamy Brie (or fresh mozzarella) cheese, cut into ¼-inch slices
- ½ cup lightly packed cilantro leaves
- 1 cup lightly packed basil leaves, sliced into thick ribbons
- ½ teaspoon kosher salt, plus more for seasoning
- ¼ teaspoon freshly cracked black pepper, plus more to taste

1. Arrange a rack 4 inches from the broiler and set it to low. In a small bowl, combine the cherries, shallots, olive oil, and vinegar and toss to combine. Arrange the bread on a small rimmed baking sheet, brush lightly with olive oil, and sprinkle with salt. Evenly distribute the cheese among the two slices of bread and broil until melted and bubbly, 5 to 7 minutes.

2. Right before the toast is done, add the cilantro, basil, salt, and pepper to the cherry-shallot mixture and gently toss to coat. Divide the salad between the toasts and drizzle any extra vinaigrette on top. Season with more salt and pepper to taste.

Zingy Broccoli & Feta Pasta

Lentil, Mango & Green Bean Salad w/ Harissa-Dijon Dressing

Preserved Lemon, Asparagus & Cherry Tomato Orzotto

Spicy Pesto, Corn & P'titim Pasta Salad

Kasha Varnishkes Salad

Perfect Rice Pilaf

Quinoa, Kohlrabi, Cabbage & Pear Salad

Salt & Pepper P'titim Tahdig

Pastas & Grains

Zingy Broccoli & Feta Pasta

SERVES 4 • ACTIVE TIME: 15 MINUTES • **TOTAL TIME:** 35 MINUTES

Dear Broccoli, sorry for all the times I took you for granted. When I lived in the United States, you were always around, reliable and ready to be put to use in my kitchen. But once I moved to Tel Aviv and realized you were actually a seasonal, ephemeral winter crop, my appreciation began to know no bounds. Now, I celebrate your versatility and value in dishes, like this easy pasta, where I tangle you with feta, parm, and lemon into a crowd-pleaser like no other. xoxo, Adeena

- 8 ounces dried spaghetti
- 6 cups (12 ounces) broccoli florets, chopped into small pieces
- ¼ cup plus 2 tablespoons olive oil
- 6 garlic cloves, thinly sliced
- 1 small jalapeño, finely chopped (3 tablespoons), seeded if desired, plus more to taste
- 1 cup (4 ounces) crumbled feta cheese, plus more for garnish
- 1 cup (1½ ounces) finely grated Parmigiano Reggiano cheese, plus more for garnish
- ½ teaspoon kosher salt, plus more for seasoning the pasta water and to taste
- ½ teaspoon freshly ground black pepper, plus more to taste
- Finely grated zest of 1 lemon (juice optional)
- ½ cup finely chopped parsley

Fill a large pot halfway with generously salted water; bring to a boil over high heat. Cook the pasta until 1 minute before al dente, reserve 1¼ cups of the pasta cooking water, add the broccoli, cook 1 additional minute, then drain the pasta and broccoli well. Heat ¼ cup of the olive oil in the same pot over medium-low heat. Add the garlic and jalapeño and cook, stirring, until the garlic is lightly golden, 2 to 3 minutes. Return the pasta and broccoli to the pot with ½ cup of the pasta water, then add the feta, parm, remaining 2 tablespoons olive oil, the salt, and pepper and warm through, adding more pasta water as needed to achieve a saucy consistency. Stir in the lemon zest (and juice, if using) and parsley and season with more salt, pepper, and jalapeño to taste. Divide among bowls and garnish with more feta and parmesan.

Lentil, Mango & Green Bean Salad w/ Harissa-Dijon Dressing

SERVES 6 TO 8 • ACTIVE TIME: 25 MINUTES • **TOTAL TIME:** 35 MINUTES

Cooking two disparate things in the same boiling water, all in the service of saving time and dishes after cooking, is a new favorite shortcut. Black lentils—also known as beluga lentils—retain a firm bite even after cooking and contain unusually high levels of antioxidants. Crisp green beans, velvety, ripe mango, a hint of mint, and crunchy red pepper are tossed in a spicy dressing that holds its own.

- 1¼ cups (9 ounces) dried black (beluga) lentils, picked over
- 12 ounces green beans, trimmed and cut into 1-inch pieces
- 6 tablespoons freshly squeezed lemon juice (from 2 lemons)
- ¼ cup olive oil
- 1 tablespoon honey
- 1 tablespoon Dijon mustard
- 1 tablespoon Harissa (page 15 or store-bought)
- 1 teaspoon kosher salt, plus more for salting the water
- ¼ teaspoon freshly ground black pepper
- 1 pound mango, cut into ½-inch cubes (1¼ cups)
- 1 red bell pepper, diced
- ½ cup diced red onion
- 1 cup lightly packed mint leaves, thinly sliced

1. Line a rimmed baking sheet with a kitchen towel. Fill a large pot halfway with generously salted water and bring to a boil over high heat. Add the lentils and cook until almost al dente, 15 minutes. Add the green beans, return to a boil, and cook until crisp-tender and bright green, 1 additional minute. Drain and rinse under cold water for 1 minute, then spread out on the towel-lined baking sheet and let sit for 10 minutes to dry and cool further.

2. In a large salad bowl, whisk together the lemon juice, olive oil, honey, mustard, harissa, ¼ teaspoon of the salt, and the pepper until creamy and lightened in color, 15 seconds. Add the lentils, green beans, mango, bell peppers, onions, and mint along with the remaining ¾ teaspoon salt; gently toss to coat.

Preserved Lemon, Asparagus & Cherry Tomato Orzotto

SERVES 4 • ACTIVE TIME: 20 MINUTES • **TOTAL TIME:** 30 MINUTES

Preparing this orzo risotto-style yields a creamy, plush pasta dish that feels rich and indulgent. The surprise here is the burst of preserved lemon, which provides a tang you don't expect from a cozy orzo dish. The springy asparagus cooks at the very end for just a few minutes, and juicy cherry tomatoes, added after the dish comes off the stove, keep things fresh. Serve as a side dish or a main course.

- ¼ cup olive oil, plus more for drizzling
- 3 garlic cloves, minced
- 1 cup dried orzo pasta
- 4 cups low-sodium vegetable broth
- ½ teaspoon kosher salt, plus more for seasoning
- 8 ounces asparagus, ends trimmed, cut into 1-inch pieces
- 1 cup (1½ ounces) finely shredded Parmigiano Reggiano cheese, plus more for garnish
- ¼ cup finely chopped Preserved Lemon (page 17 or store-bought) from ½ small preserved lemon)
- ½ teaspoon dried red pepper flakes
- Freshly ground black pepper
- 1 cup cherry tomatoes, quartered

Heat the olive oil in a medium saucepan over medium-low heat. Add the garlic and cook, stirring, until fragrant, 1 to 2 minutes. Add the orzo and cook, stirring, until glossy, 2 minutes. Stir in the broth and salt, raise the heat to medium-high, and bring to a low boil. Reduce the heat to medium-low and simmer, stirring every few minutes, until the orzo is just cooked through but still very soupy, 13 minutes. Stir in the asparagus, return to a simmer, and cook until the asparagus is al dente, 2 minutes. Stir in the parm, preserved lemon, and red pepper flakes. Divide among four plates, top each plate with ¼ cup of the tomatoes, drizzle with olive oil, and garnish with more cheese.

Spicy Pesto, Corn & P'titim Pasta Salad

SERVES 6 • ACTIVE TIME: 20 MINUTES **• TOTAL TIME:** 30 MINUTES

If you love pasta salads but don't love how they swallow up flavor—leaving you with bland, sad noodles—this one's for you. Quick-cooking p'titim (Israel's version of fregola, maftoul, or pearl couscous) are the ideal vehicle for mildly spicy pesto, which coats every bite with green goodness. The jumble of mozzarella, tomatoes, pine nuts, and onions makes this one picnic-worthy. Also great for packed lunches for both adults and kids.

⅔ cup pine nuts

2 cups fresh basil leaves, plus more for garnish

1 cup (1½ ounces) finely grated Parmigiano Reggiano cheese

½ cup olive oil

3 garlic cloves, chopped

½ small jalapeño (seeded, if desired)

1 teaspoon kosher salt, plus more for salting the water and to taste

½ teaspoon freshly ground black pepper, plus more to taste

1½ cups dried p'titim (Israeli/pearl couscous)

2½ cups fresh corn kernels (from 3 ears corn, or equal amount frozen and thawed, or canned and drained)

1½ cups cherry tomatoes, quartered

½ cup diced red onion

1 cup (6 ounces) fresh mini mozzarella balls (or cubed fresh mozzarella)

⅓ cup pitted kalamata or other olives, chopped

1. Preheat the oven to 350°F. Bring a large pot of generously salted water to a boil over high heat. Arrange the pine nuts on a small rimmed baking sheet and toast until lightly golden, 6 to 7 minutes; cool on the sheet pan.

2. Make the pesto: In a bullet-style blender or food processor, combine the basil, parm, olive oil, half of the toasted pine nuts, garlic, jalapeño, ½ teaspoon of the salt, and ¼ teaspoon of the pepper and blend or pulse until creamy and thick (makes a scant cup; pesto can be refrigerated in an airtight container for up to 5 days, or frozen in ice cube trays for up to 6 months).

3. Add the p'titim to the boiling water and cook according to the package directions. Two minutes before al dente add the corn, return to a boil, and cook until the pasta is al dente and the corn is tender-crisp, 2 minutes. Drain and rinse the p'titim and corn thoroughly under cold water (you can pat dry with a kitchen towel if desired), then transfer to a large bowl. Add the pesto, tomatoes, onions, mozzarella, olives, remaining pine nuts, remaining ½ teaspoon salt, and remaining ¼ teaspoon pepper and toss to coat. Toss in a few fresh basil leaves and season with more salt and pepper to taste.

4. Serve immediately or chill if desired; this salad can be refrigerated in an airtight container for up to 3 days.

Kasha Varnishkes Salad

SERVES 5 • ACTIVE TIME: 20 MINUTES • **TOTAL TIME:** 45 MINUTES

The original version of this—a sort of grain-and-pasta pilaf with eastern European roots made with buckwheat groats (kasha) and bow tie noodles (varnishkes)—was always on the table at every Shabbat and holiday in our home growing up. My mom often used the Wolff's brand box, which was a sort of beacon of Ashkenazi culture often available in the tiny kosher section of local supermarkets. I update it here into a bright pasta salad with spicy radishes, bitter greens, and roasted mushrooms. The dressing makes all the ingredients in this salad stand up and pay attention.

- 1½ teaspoons kosher salt, plus more for seasoning
- 4 ounces (1½ cups) dried bow tie pasta
- ½ cup dried kasha (buckwheat groats)
- ½ cup olive oil, plus more as needed
- 1¼ pounds mixed mushrooms, cleaned, stemmed, and quartered
- 1 tablespoon Dijon mustard
- ¼ cup distilled white vinegar
- 1 teaspoon sugar
- ¼ teaspoon coarsely ground black pepper
- ½ medium red onion, sliced
- 4 small radishes, thinly sliced (½ cup)
- One 5-ounce package (5 cups loosely packed) baby arugula leaves

1. Preheat the oven to 450°F. Fill a large saucepan halfway with generously salted water and bring to a boil over high heat. Add the pasta and kasha and boil until cooked, 11 to 12 minutes. Drain the pasta and kasha well, add to a large salad bowl, and toss with a splash of olive oil to prevent sticking.

2. Arrange the mushrooms on a sheet pan and drizzle with ¼ cup of the olive oil and 1 teaspoon of the salt; toss to coat. Roast until the mushrooms have browned and reduced in size, 14 to 15 minutes.

3. In a salad bowl, whisk the remaining ¼ cup olive oil with the mustard, vinegar, sugar, pepper, and remaining ½ teaspoon salt. Add the mushrooms, onions, radishes, and reserved pasta and kasha and toss to coat. Before serving, add the arugula and toss.

Perfect Rice Pilaf

SERVES 6 TO 8 • ACTIVE TIME: 20 MINUTES **• TOTAL TIME:** 40 MINUTES

This is the last rice side dish you'll ever need. The tender onions and carrots, the generous amount of cumin and paprika, and the perfectly cooked rice add up to a pilaf that goes with so many meals. Somehow it manages to be flavor-packed and neutral at the same time. I add herbs at the end (oops, we forgot them in this photo, which is gorgeous anyway!); swap in any herb of your choice.

- 2 cups long-grain rice, such as basmati, jasmine, or Persian
- 3 tablespoons olive oil
- 1 large onion, finely diced
- 1 large carrot, finely diced
- 2 tablespoons tomato paste
- 2 garlic cloves, minced
- 1 tablespoon sweet paprika
- 1½ teaspoons ground cumin
- 3½ cups low-sodium vegetable broth or water, plus ¼ cup if needed
- 2 teaspoons kosher salt, plus more to taste
- ¼ cup chopped parsley

If using jasmine or Persian rice, rinse the rice under cold running water until the water runs clear, 30 to 45 seconds; drain well. Heat the oil in a large saucepan over medium heat. Add the onions and carrots and cook, stirring, until the onions are lightly golden and the carrots are tender, 8 to 9 minutes. Add the tomato paste, garlic, paprika, and cumin and cook, stirring, until fragrant, 2 minutes. Stir in the rice and cook, stirring, until it turns red, 1 to 2 minutes. Add the broth and salt, bring to a boil, reduce the heat to a simmer, cover, and cook until the rice is tender and no liquid remains, 17 to 18 minutes. Uncover and taste a grain of rice. If the rice seems al dente, add ¼ cup of water, re-cover, and continue to cook until tender, an extra 2 minutes. Remove from the heat and let rest, covered, for 5 minutes. Uncover, transfer to a serving bowl, stir in the parsley, and season with more salt to taste.

Quinoa, Kohlrabi, Cabbage & Pear Salad

SERVES 6 TO 8 • ACTIVE TIME: 40 MINUTES • **TOTAL TIME:** 1 HOUR

If you have any preconceived notions about quinoa, you may reconsider them after making this crunchy, nutty, satisfying salad, chockablock with fruit, veggies, and roasted nuts. Half the deal is just cooking the quinoa properly; don't use too much water, then if it still feels waterlogged, use my method of stirring the pot with the lid open at the end to evaporate extra moisture. Finally, spreading the quinoa on a sheet pan helps it dry out even further as it cools.

1 cup raw almonds

⅓ cup plus 1 tablespoon olive oil

1¼ cups uncooked quinoa, rinsed and drained

1 teaspoon kosher salt, plus more to taste

2½ cups water

3 tablespoons red wine vinegar

1½ tablespoons Dijon mustard

1½ tablespoons silan (date syrup) or honey

½ teaspoon freshly ground black pepper, plus more to taste

¼ small (8-ounce) head red cabbage, shredded (4 cups)*

1 large or 2 small kohlrabi or jicama, peeled and sliced into matchsticks

2 medium very firm pears, thinly sliced

½ small red onion, thinly sliced

1. Preheat the oven to 350°F. Arrange the almonds on a small rimmed baking sheet; toast until fragrant and golden, 10 minutes. Cool and coarsely chop.

2. In a medium, wide saucepan with a lid, heat 1 tablespoon of the olive oil over medium heat. Add the quinoa and ½ teaspoon of the salt and toast, stirring, 2 to 3 minutes. Add the water, raise the heat to high, and bring to a boil. Reduce the heat to low and simmer, covered, until all the water is absorbed and the quinoa is soft, 20 to 25 minutes. Remove from the heat and let stand, covered, for 5 minutes (if the quinoa is still wet, cook, uncovered, over medium heat, stirring, to evaporate any extra moisture, 3 to 4 minutes). Transfer to a large rimmed baking sheet and spread in an even layer to cool completely.

3. In a large salad bowl, whisk together the remaining ⅓ cup olive oil, the vinegar, mustard, silan, the remaining ½ teaspoon salt, and the pepper until creamy. Add the quinoa, almonds, cabbage, kohlrabi, pears, and onions and toss to combine. Season with salt and pepper.

**If desired, swap 2 cups of the cabbage for shredded radicchio.*

Salt & Pepper P'titim Tahdig

SERVES 6 • ACTIVE TIME: 10 MINUTES **• TOTAL TIME:** 35 MINUTES

I clearly can't get enough of p'titim, so I found a great new way to serve them: crisped up into a sort of tahdig-inspired crispy-bottomed starchy side dish. But in this case the rice is switched with these tiny orbs of pasta. To replace the usual yogurt and keep this dish dairy-free, I mixed an egg into the cooked p'titim before returning them to the oiled pan. The proteins in the egg bind the bottom of the rice into a crispy fried shell, creating the texture for which the dish is known (and named).

6 cups water

1½ tablespoons kosher salt, plus more to taste

½ teaspoon ground turmeric

3 cups p'titim (Israeli/pearl couscous)

1 large egg, beaten

½ teaspoon coarsely ground black pepper, plus more to taste

¼ cup olive oil

Bring the water, 1 tablespoon of the salt, and the turmeric to a boil in a medium saucepan. Add the p'titim, return to a boil, and cook until al dente, 6 minutes. Drain, rinse, and drain again until relatively dry, 5 to 10 minutes. Combine in a bowl with the egg, the remaining 1½ teaspoons salt, and the pepper. Arrange a large, clean kitchen towel on the counter. Place the lid of a 9-inch nonstick skillet in the center of the towel, bring the ends of the towel to meet on top of the lid, and tie them so the lid is wrapped in the towel. Heat the oil in the skillet over medium-high heat. Pour the p'titim mixture into the pan, spreading it out to the sides. Cover and cook for 3 minutes, then reduce the heat to medium and cook until the edges of the tahdig are deep golden brown and the underside is crisp, 9 to 10 minutes. Uncover and place an inverted plate slightly larger than the diameter of the skillet over the top. Use oven mitts to flip the tahdig onto the plate; it should be deep golden brown and crispy on top. Season with more salt and pepper to taste.

Pink Grapefruit, Arak & Thyme Cooler

Cherry Basil Ginger Smash

Spicy Watermelon Whiskey Sour

Sweet & Salty Bissli Brittle

Frozen Melon Lime-O-Nana

Tel Aviv Sunrise

Savory Spiced Popcorn

Drinks

Pink Grapefruit, Arak & Thyme Cooler

MAKES 4 DRINKS (WITH LEFTOVER SYRUP) • ACTIVE TIME: 10 MINUTES
TOTAL TIME (INCLUDING SYRUP COOLING): 30 MINUTES

I bought a bottle of beautiful Jordanian arak from Zahi Greib at his shop in Nazareth, known for its prodigious selection of anise-scented spirits from all over the levant and Middle East. In its commercial mass-produced form, arak has about as much subtlety as paint thinner. But get yourself a quality bottle and you can almost taste the anise seeds being distilled into the alcohol. To me there's no fruit more perfect for pairing with arak than pink grapefruit; its gorgeous color and piquant-sweet flavor combo holds its own with the arak, which tends to show up strong. Use any extra thyme-peppercorn syrup to sweeten tea, or to drizzle over fruit.

- ½ cup sugar
- 4 ounces (½ cup) water
- 10 whole black peppercorns
- 8 thyme sprigs (halved if very long), plus more for garnish
- Fine sea salt or pink Himalayan salt
- 8 ounces (1 cup) pink grapefruit juice (preferably freshly squeezed, from 1 large grapefruit), plus thin grapefruit slices for garnish
- 4 ounces (½ cup) arak, Pernod, or other anise-scented spirit

1. Combine the sugar, water, peppercorns, thyme, and a pinch of salt in a small saucepan. Bring to a boil over medium-high heat, reduce to low, and simmer until the sugar dissolves completely and the mixture thickens slightly, 2 to 3 minutes. Remove from the heat and transfer everything to a small jar (you will have ¾ cup syrup). Cool completely (syrup will continue to develop flavor if you leave everything in the jar, and will last in the fridge for up to 3 months).

2. In an ice-filled cocktail shaker, combine the grapefruit juice, arak, and ¼ cup simple syrup; shake vigorously for 10 seconds, then strain into four ice-filled rocks glasses. Garnish with grapefruit slices and thyme sprigs.

عرق إكسترا مثلث

Cherry Basil Ginger Smash

MAKES 2 DRINKS • ACTIVE TIME: 10 MINUTES • **TOTAL TIME:** 10 MINUTES

We recently started growing basil on our porch (we're not cherry-level gardeners yet), and this cocktail puts my favorite summer herb to good use in a gingery mash-up. To make this in larger proportions, mix all the ingredients in a pitcher without ice, stir vigorously, then pour over ice when ready to serve.

- 2½ limes
- 1½ tablespoons (¾ ounce) honey
- 1 thin slice fresh ginger
- 1 small basil sprig, plus more leaves for garnish
- ⅔ cup (about 15 large/ 4 ounces) red cherries, pitted
- 4 ounces (½ cup) gin
- 1½ cups ice, plus more to top off glasses
- 4 ounces (½ cup) seltzer

Juice 1½ of the limes (you should have 3 to 4 tablespoons juice), then cut the remaining half into 4 rounds. In a cocktail shaker, combine the lime juice, 2 lime rounds, the honey, ginger, and basil sprig and use a cocktail muddler to mash the ginger and lime. Add the cherries and muddle until mashed, 5 seconds. Add the gin and ice, seal the shaker, and shake vigorously for 10 to 15 seconds. Remove and discard the smashed lime rounds and ginger slice, divide the cocktail and ice between two highball glasses, add ¼ cup more ice to each glass, top each glass with seltzer, then garnish with lime rounds and basil leaves.

Frozen Melon Lime-O-Nana

MAKES 4 DRINKS • ACTIVE TIME: 15 MINUTES
TOTAL TIME (INCLUDING FREEZING TIME): 2 HOURS 15 MINUTES

In a classic Israeli frozen limonana, mint, lemon, sugar, and ice are blended into a tart-and-sweet slushy that brings summer to the glass year-round. This recipe is a greener, lime-centric version that incorporates frozen cubes of lush, ripe green melon with less ice for a more concentrated, extremely flavor-packed version.

- 1 pound juicy honeydew or other green melon, cut into chunks
- 2 large limes
- 6 ounces (¾ cup) vodka
- ⅓ cup sugar
- ½ cup packed mint leaves, plus mint for garnish
- 1 cup ice

1. Arrange the melon in a single layer on a plastic wrap–lined plate or small baking sheet. Freeze until partially solid, 1 to 2 hours (or freeze longer and thaw until the melon is mostly hard but can be pierced with a toothpick, 15 minutes).

2. Use a peeler to peel the zest into thick strips from half of one of the limes. Juice both limes (you should have ⅓ cup juice). Transfer the frozen melon to a blender with the lime strips, vodka, lime juice, and sugar and blend until almost smooth, 15 to 20 seconds. Add the mint and ice and blend until you see small green flecks in the drink and the ice is almost smooth, 10 to 15 more seconds. Divide the drink among four glasses.

Spicy Watermelon Whiskey Sour w/ Sweet & Salty Bissli Brittle

MAKES 2 DRINKS • ACTIVE TIME: 10 MINUTES • **TOTAL TIME:** 10 MINUTES

Making your own watermelon juice is easy; just blend and strain. Then you have the base for this spicy refresher (the jalapeño sneaks up on you!) anytime. A basic good whiskey works wonders here (Jay always has some Jack Daniel's around). I would avoid swapping in smoky scotch, whose flavors may overpower the drink. The brittle, made with an Israeli snack-food staple, is a sophisticated guilty pleasure that you'll find hard to resist.

- 2½ cups (12 ounces) cubed watermelon*
- 2 teaspoons diced seeded jalapeño (preferably red), or ¼ teaspoon cayenne
- 4 ounces (½ cup) whiskey or bourbon
- 3 ounces (6 tablespoons) fresh lemon juice
- 2 tablespoons (1 ounce) honey
- Large mint sprig, plus more for garnish

In a blender, combine the watermelon and jalapeño and blend until smooth, 15 to 20 seconds. Strain through a fine-mesh strainer, discarding the solids; you should have a generous cup of liquid. In a cocktail shaker (or a large jar with a lid), combine the spicy watermelon juice, whiskey, lemon juice, honey, and mint and shake vigorously (with no ice, to help the honey dissolve). Fill two rocks glasses with ice and divide the cocktail between the glasses. Garnish with mint sprigs.

**Can be replaced with 1¼ cups store-bought watermelon juice, such as WTRMLN or Pure Green.*

Sweet & Salty Bissli Brittle

MAKES ABOUT 1½ CUPS • ACTIVE TIME: 5 MINUTES
TOTAL TIME (INCLUDING COOLING TIME): 35 MINUTES

Invented in Israel in the 1970s when a factory manager threw some pasta into a deep fryer, deeply crunchy Bissli has grown to become one of Israel's most popular snacks, with multiple flavors and shapes. I balance its salty grill seasoning by making a quick caramel, which binds the Bissli and a bunch of other salty snacks together into snackable clusters. Though I specifically call for the spiral-shaped Bissli, any shape or flavor can be swapped in.

- 3 tablespoons maple syrup
- 1 tablespoon olive oil
- ¼ teaspoon dried red pepper flakes or cayenne
- ¼ teaspoon kosher salt, plus more to taste
- ½ cup Bissli Grill flavored snack*
- ¼ cup toasted corn snacks, such as Corn Nuts
- ¼ cup wasabi peas
- ¼ cup roasted shelled peanuts (salted or unsalted)

1. Preheat the oven to 300°F. Line a rimmed baking sheet with parchment paper. In a medium bowl, vigorously whisk the maple syrup, oil, dried red pepper flakes, and salt until lightened in color, 30 seconds. Add the Bissli, corn snacks, wasabi peas, and peanuts and gently toss to coat completely, 15 seconds. Transfer to the prepared baking sheet and spread in a single layer (it's OK for pieces to be touching). Bake, stirring once midway through, until the caramel darkens in color and bubbles, 25 to 20 minutes. Cool completely and break into clusters.

2. Store in an airtight container for up to 1 week.

**Bissli Grill is available in kosher and some Middle Eastern grocers. Any other Bissli flavor or shape will do, as will Fritos Honey BBQ Flavor Twists.*

Savory Spiced Popcorn

MAKES 8 CUPS • **ACTIVE TIME:** 5 MINUTES • **TOTAL TIME:** 10 MINUTES

Nutritional yeast adds the perfect "cheesy" flavor here, or you can make it dairy by using the plastic-jarred, powdery parm you find in the supermarket. I always try to start with homemade oil-popped popcorn (I put the instructions below), but store-bought works just fine. Though I suggest serving this with my Tel Aviv Sunrise cocktail (see page 224), it goes with practically any drink you can think of. I go heavy on the pepper, but feel free to lighten up on the spice there.

- ⅓ cup nutritional yeast flakes (or supermarket-style grated parmesan cheese)
- ½ teaspoon freshly cracked black pepper (or less, if desired)
- ½ teaspoon ground cumin
- ¼ teaspoon ground turmeric
- ¼ teaspoon smoked or sweet paprika
- ¼ teaspoon fine sea salt
- 8 cups popped plain popcorn, store-bought or oil-popped*
- 2 tablespoons olive oil

1. In a small bowl combine the nutritional yeast, pepper, cumin, turmeric, paprika, and salt.

2. Put the popcorn in a large bowl, drizzle with the olive oil, and use salad tongs to toss and coat the popcorn well with the oil, 15 to 20 seconds. Add the spice mixture and use the tongs to toss well to coat, another 10 to 15 seconds.

**To make homemade popcorn (makes 8 cups): Heat 3 tablespoons neutral oil and 2 kernels unpopped popcorn in a medium lidded saucepan over medium-high heat. Once the kernels pop, add ⅓ cup popcorn kernels, cover with the lid, and cook, shaking gently, until the kernels pop, then stop popping, 1 to 2 minutes. Uncover and transfer to a bowl.*

Tel Aviv Sunrise

MAKES 1 DRINK* • ACTIVE TIME: 5 MINUTES **• TOTAL TIME:** 5 MINUTES

2 ounces (¼ cup) pomegranate juice

4 ounces (½ cup) orange juice, plus orange slices for garnish

1½ ounces (3 tablespoons) blanco or silver tequila

3 or 4 drops classic or citrus cocktail bitters

Here in the Carmel Market, pomegranates are still in season when juicy-sweet oranges begin to make their appearance. This dead-simple drink fuses both to great effect—visually and tastewise. A little tequila turns this into a local version of the classic Mexican-inspired cocktail. Serve with Savory Spiced Popcorn (page 223) for the ideal salty snack accompaniment.

Pour the pomegranate juice into a highball (tall) glass, then carefully fill the glass to the top with ice. In a measuring cup, combine the orange juice, tequila, and bitters and slowly pour the mixture into the glass; there should be a bright crimson layer and an orange layer. Garnish with an orange slice.

**To make 4 drinks in a 2-quart pitcher: Start with 8 ounces (1 cup) pomegranate juice, 16 ounces (2 cups) orange juice, and 6 ounces (¾ cup) tequila. Add bitters to taste and divide among ice-filled glasses.*

Desserts

Medjool Date Bundt Cake w/ Clementine Glaze

Pistachio Carrot Cake w/ Labaneh Frosting

One-Bowl Summer Fruit Cake

No-Bake Tahini Cheesecake

Chocolate-Cardamom Snacking Cake

Bamba PB Marshmallow Treats

Coconut Creamsicle Malabi

Tangy Lime Blondies

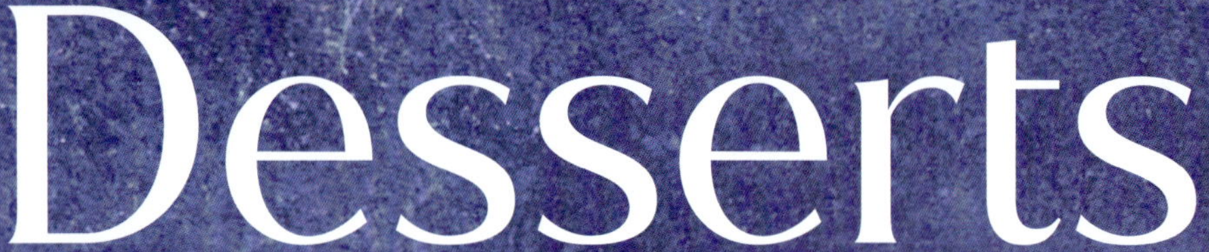

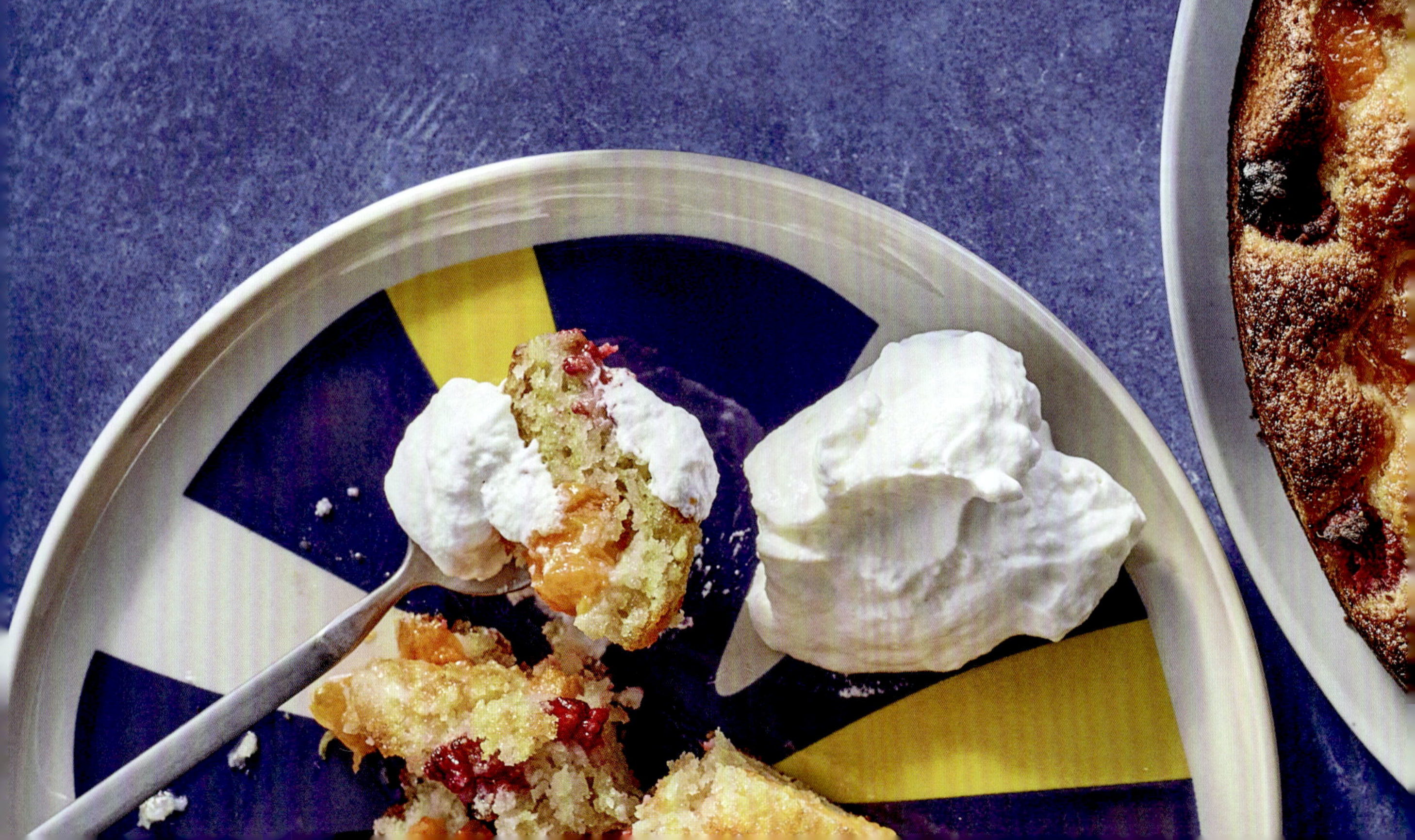

Medjool Date Bundt Cake w/ Clementine Glaze

SERVES 12 • ACTIVE TIME: 15 MINUTES **• TOTAL TIME:** 70 MINUTES

My dear friend Mickey Perez, owner of the beloved Caffe Tamati (see photo, page 245) near my home, bakes cakes that he sells by the slice near the register. His date Bundt cake, simultaneously dense and light with hints of caramel, captivated me. In Israel, date paste is as easy to find as peanut butter, but I start with whole dates; if you can find date paste, by all means use it. As the cake sits on the counter, it gets plusher by the day, absolutely perfect for any coffee break. I added a citrusy glaze, though it's totally delicious on its own.

- Cooking spray
- 20 to 21 large Medjool dates (15 ounces/440 grams), pitted and finely chopped*
- 1⅔ cups (295 ml/grams) boiling water
- 1 teaspoon instant espresso or strong coffee powder
- 5 large eggs
- 1 tablespoon (15 ml/grams) pure vanilla extract
- 1⅔ cups (275 grams) lightly packed dark brown sugar
- 1 cup neutral oil
- 2¼ cups (295 grams) all-purpose flour
- 2½ teaspoons (10 grams) baking powder
- 1 teaspoon (5 grams) baking soda
- ¾ teaspoon (5 grams) fine sea salt, plus more for the glaze
- 2 cups (250 grams) confectioners' sugar
- ¼ cup (60 ml) clementine juice and 1 tablespoon finely grated zest (from 1 large clementine), plus more zest for garnish

Arrange a rack in the center of the oven; preheat to 350°F. Generously coat a standard Bundt pan with cooking spray (or vegetable oil). In the bowl of a stand mixer or in a large bowl, combine the dates, boiling water, and coffee powder. Let sit until the dates have softened to the consistency of chunky applesauce, 10 minutes. Beat with the paddle attachment (or an electric hand mixer or a large whisk and a strong arm) on medium speed until almost smooth, 30 seconds. Add the eggs and vanilla and beat until well blended, 20 seconds. Add the brown sugar and oil and beat until blended, 10 more seconds. Reduce the speed to low and beat in the flour, baking powder, baking soda, and salt until just incorporated, 20 seconds. Transfer the batter to the prepared pan and bake until a tester comes out clean and the top is dark golden, 45 to 55 minutes. Cool in the pan for 20 to 25 minutes; the cake will shrink away from the sides a bit as it cools. Use a thin knife to loosen the cake from the pan, tilting and applying light pressure as you work your way around the outside and center of the cake. Then say your Bundt Cake Release Prayer and invert onto a serving plate to cool. In a medium bowl, whisk the confectioners' sugar, clementine juice and zest, and a very generous pinch of salt until smooth. Pour half the glaze over the cooled cake, let sit for 5 minutes, then pour the remaining glaze over the cake. Garnish with more clementine zest.

**Dates can be swapped for 14 oz/400 grams date paste. Simply add the boiling water and coffee to the date paste instead of the whole pitted dates.*

Pistachio Carrot Cake w/ Labaneh Frosting

SERVES 12 • ACTIVE TIME: 20 MINUTES
TOTAL TIME (INCLUDING COOLING AND FROSTING): 2 HOURS

No fussy layers here. Packed with raisins and studded with pistachios, this cinnamony carrot snacking cake is as juicy as it gets. A generous amount of oil helps with the moist crumb, and the labaneh frosting gives just the right amount of creamy tartness. You can prepare the frosting and cake separately in advance, then frost just before serving if you like. To keep the cake dairy-free, swap in a vegan Greek yogurt or cream cheese.

1 cup (240 ml/210 grams) neutral oil, plus more for greasing the pan

1 cup (240 grams/ml) full-fat labaneh or Greek yogurt

1½ cups (318 grams) lightly packed light brown sugar

2 large eggs

2 teaspoons (10 grams/ml) pure vanilla extract or paste

2 teaspoons (8 grams) ground cinnamon

1½ teaspoons (6 grams) baking soda

½ teaspoon (3 grams) kosher salt, plus more for the frosting

1½ cups (195 grams) all-purpose flour

2½ cups (240 grams) coarsely grated carrots (from 2 large or 3 medium carrots)

1 cup (130 grams) golden raisins

1¼ cups (200 grams) shelled roasted pistachios, coarsely chopped (salted is fine)

¾ cup (95 grams) confectioners' sugar

1. Preheat the oven to 350°F. Grease an 8-inch square baking pan with oil.

2. Line a fine-mesh strainer with a triple layer of cheesecloth or a clean towel, add the labaneh, and let it drain in the fridge while you make the cake.

3. In a large bowl, vigorously whisk the brown sugar, oil, eggs, and vanilla until creamy and incorporated, 1 minute. Whisk in the cinnamon, baking soda, and salt, then fold in the flour with a spatula or wooden spoon until just incorporated (a few streaks or lumps are OK). Fold in the carrots, raisins, and 1 cup of the pistachios. Transfer the batter to the prepared pan; bake until the center is set and the top is lightly golden, 45 to 50 minutes. Remove from the oven and cool completely in the pan. When the cake is cool, in a medium bowl, whisk the labaneh and confectioners' sugar with a pinch of salt until smooth and creamy, 30 to 45 seconds. Spread the frosting evenly across the cake. Finely chop the remaining ¼ cup pistachios, sprinkle on top of the cake, and cut into 12 squares.

One-Bowl Summer Fruit Cake

SERVES 8 • ACTIVE TIME: 20 MINUTES • **TOTAL TIME:** 1 HOUR 30 MINUTES

Just sweet enough and packed with fruit, this low-investment, high-reward dessert is the cake you'll make on repeat. Almond meal and labaneh create a super-tender crumb, and the very accommodating batter welcomes pretty much any stone fruit or berry you have on hand. Make sure you only partially melt the butter as instructed; it helps the cake maintain its light, yet moist, structure.

- 1 stick (4 ounces/113 grams) unsalted butter, cubed, plus more for greasing the pan
- 1 cup (200 grams) plus 2 tablespoons (26 grams) sugar
- 2 large eggs
- ⅔ cup (135 grams) plus ½ cup (100 grams) labaneh, sour cream, or full-fat Greek yogurt
- 2 teaspoons finely grated lemon zest
- 1½ teaspoons (8 ml) pure vanilla extract
- 1 cup (130 grams) all-purpose flour
- ¾ cup (75 grams) fine almond meal
- 1½ teaspoons (7 grams) baking powder
- ¼ teaspoon (1 gram) kosher salt
- 1 pound (450 grams) very ripe stone fruit (peaches, plums, apricots), pitted and sliced
- ⅔ cup (55 grams) raspberries
- ⅔ cup (160 ml) heavy cream

Preheat the oven to 350°F. Grease a 9- or 10-inch Springform pan with butter. In a large microwave-safe bowl, microwave the butter in 10- or 15-second increments until the butter slumps but is still mostly opaque with a few melted spots, 25 to 30 seconds. Add 1 cup of the sugar and use the biggest whisk you have (or an electric hand mixer) to beat the butter and sugar (the first few seconds may be tough, but it will get easier) until light and fluffy, 1 to 2 minutes. Add the eggs, ⅔ cup labaneh, lemon zest, and vanilla to the bowl and beat until fluffy, 1 minute. Add the flour, almond meal, baking powder, and salt and fold in until just combined, 10 to 15 seconds. Transfer the batter to the prepared pan, then distribute the stone fruit and berries evenly over the top, followed by 1 tablespoon of the sugar. Bake until the fruit is cooked and slumped and the top is lightly golden, 40 to 45 minutes. Cool and slice. While the cake is cooling, in a medium bowl whisk the whipped cream with the remaining ½ cup labaneh and remaining 2 tablespoons sugar until soft peaks form, 2 minutes. Serve the labaneh whipped cream with the cake.

No-Bake Tahini Cheesecake

SERVES 10 • ACTIVE TIME: 15 MINUTES
TOTAL TIME (INCLUDING MINIMUM CHILLING TIME): 5 HOURS 15 MINUTES

Yes, a cheesecake you don't bake can be just as good as one that you do—and here is the proof. The secret is to make sure your dairy products are drained of excess liquid, and to use the full amount of tahini, a magical substance that, when chilled, helps the cake firm up without any eggs. Biscoff cookies (the same ones you find on Delta flights) form the base of the buttery, sweet-salty, no-bake crust. Crown with raspberries for a very special dessert.

- 5 tablespoons (2¼ ounces/65 grams) unsalted butter, melted
- One (8.8-ounce) package (about 32) Lotus (Biscoff) cookies
- 1½ tablespoons (20 grams) light or dark brown sugar
- ¼ teaspoon (1 gram) kosher salt
- ¾ cup (180 grams/ml) heavy whipping cream
- 1¾ pounds (800 grams) full-fat brick-style cream cheese, drained of any excess liquid
- 1½ cups full-fat labaneh or Greek yogurt, drained of any excess liquid
- 1¾ cups (245 grams) confectioners' sugar
- 3 tablespoons (21 grams) cornstarch
- 1½ teaspoons (8 grams/ml) pure vanilla extract
- 1 cup (250 grams/240 ml) tahini paste
- ½ cup raspberries

Brush the bottom and sides of a 9-inch springform pan with a bit of the melted butter, then line the bottom with parchment paper. Reserve 4 cookies. Place the remaining 28 cookies in a large Ziploc bag and seal; bash and roll with a rolling pin until fine crumbs form, 30 seconds. Add the butter, brown sugar, and ⅛ teaspoon of the salt to the bag, reseal, and shake until the crumbs are coated. Press firmly into the bottom of the pan; transfer to the freezer while you make the filling. In the bowl of a stand mixer fitted with the whisk attachment, beat the cream on medium-high speed until stiff peaks form, 2 to 3 minutes. Scrape the whipped cream into a separate bowl, then add the cream cheese, labaneh, confectioners' sugar, cornstarch, vanilla, and the remaining ⅛ teaspoon salt to the mixer bowl. Beat on high until fluffy, 2 to 3 minutes. Reduce the speed to low, whisk in the tahini, then stop the mixer and fold in the whipped cream by hand. Remove the crust from the freezer, spread the mixture evenly over the crust, cover with plastic wrap, and chill for at least 5 hours, but preferably overnight. Uncover, run a hot knife around the edges of the pan, release the cake, transfer to a serving dish, and top with the raspberries. Crumble the reserved 4 cookies over the top and cut the cake into 10 equal-sized wedges.

Chocolate-Cardamom Snacking Cake

SERVES 12 • ACTIVE TIME: 15 MINUTES **• TOTAL TIME:** 55 MINUTES

I wanted this no-mixer cake to be lickety-split simple, deeply chocolate flavored, and—somewhat impossibly—light and rich at the same time. To achieve chocolate nirvana, use the best cocoa you can find; here I chose natural cocoa powder (most store-bought brands are), which reacts well with the acidic baking soda and coffee in this recipe and also has a deeper, more chocolatey flavor than so-called Dutch-process cocoa, from which the acidity has been removed by an alkali. I added cardamom for flavor, but by incorporating hot coffee—which I did for the moisture and depth it lends—I now realize this is yet another take on my Turkish coffee cold brew, which I adore. As soon as the tester comes out clean, remove this baby from the oven to avoid any dryness. And if you have the patience (or leftovers), you'll find this one gets more tender by the day.

- ½ cup (120 ml) neutral oil, plus more for greasing the pan
- 1½ cups (195 grams) all-purpose flour
- ⅔ cup (60 grams) cocoa powder
- 2 teaspoons (11 grams) baking soda
- 1 teaspoon (5 grams) baking powder
- 1½ teaspoons (5 grams) ground cardamom
- ½ teaspoon (3 grams) fine sea salt
- ½ cup (120 grams/ml) almond milk (or other milk)
- 1⅓ cups (266 grams) granulated sugar
- 2 large eggs
- 2 teaspoons (10 grams/ml) pure vanilla extract or paste
- 1 tablespoon (7 grams) instant coffee powder (or 2 teaspoons espresso powder)
- ¾ cup (180 ml/grams) boiling or very hot tap water
- Confectioners' sugar, for dusting

1. Preheat the oven to 350°F. Grease a 9-inch square baking pan lightly with oil.

2. In a large bowl, whisk the flour, cocoa, baking soda, baking powder, cardamom, and salt.

3. In a medium bowl, whisk the almond milk with the granulated sugar, oil, eggs, and vanilla, then gently whisk the wet ingredients into the dry until incorporated; a few streaks are fine. Dissolve the instant coffee in the boiling water, then gently whisk it into the batter (the batter will be thin). Pour the batter into the prepared pan and bake until puffed and a tester comes out with dry crumbs, 35 to 40 minutes. Cool completely, then dust with confectioners' sugar.

Bamba PB Marshmallow Treats

MAKES 16 BARS • ACTIVE TIME: 10 MINUTES **• TOTAL TIME:** 25 MINUTES

Did you know that virtually no Israeli children have peanut allergies? It's largely because of Bamba, a ubiquitous peanut puff (think savory cheese doodle) that is often among a baby's first foods in this part of the world. Many adults love them, too—especially those like me who adore peanut butter. You can find them at kosher stores and, since 2017, at Trader Joe's, who bought the proprietary recipe and produces the snack in the United States. Here, I let Rice Krispies Treats be my inspiration, mixing the Bamba with melted marshmallows and a generous lashing of salt before pressing into a pan and adorning with a chocolate drizzle.

3 tablespoons (42 grams) butter or coconut oil

One 10-ounce (285 grams) package large marshmallows

One 3.5-ounce bag (about 5½ cups) Bamba peanut puffs*

1 teaspoon (3 grams) flaky sea salt, such as Maldon

Cooking spray

¼ cup (42 grams) semisweet chocolate chips

1 teaspoon (5 grams) neutral or coconut oil

Line a 9-inch square pan with parchment paper. Melt the butter in a large high-sided pot over low heat. Add the marshmallows and warm them, stirring, until just fully melted, 2 to 3 minutes. Remove from the heat and, working quickly, stir in the Bamba and ½ teaspoon of the salt until fully coated. Again, working fast, transfer the mixture to the prepared pan. Let cool slightly, then spray your hands with cooking spray and press the mixture down slightly to even out and fill out the pan. Chill for 10 minutes. In a small, microwave-safe bowl, combine the chocolate chips and neutral oil and microwave, stopping every 30 seconds to stir, until melted and drizzleable, 1 minute. Remove the pan from the fridge, drizzle the chocolate mixture over the top, sprinkle with the remaining ½ teaspoon salt, and freeze for 5 minutes to solidify the chocolate. Cut into 16 equal-sized squares. Store in the fridge in an airtight container for up to 1 week.

**Available at Trader Joe's or kosher/Israeli markets.*

Coconut Creamsicle Malabi

SERVES 6 • ACTIVE TIME: 20 MINUTES
TOTAL TIME (INCLUDING CHILLING TIME): 2 HOURS 20 MINUTES

There's a reason malabi—the creamy, cornstarch-thickened, pudding-like dessert with origins in Turkey—is so popular in Tel Aviv restaurants. Once you get the formula right, it's easy to make and holds in the fridge for a good three to four days. I do everything in one saucepan, starting with cold ingredients that I whisk off the heat before bringing up to a boil. It's a method I learned from Clio Goodman, a Brooklyn bakery owner whose pudding-centric cookbook I had the honor of working on many years ago. Adding lots of vanilla makes the coconut base positively floral, and the orange simple syrup—with an optional pinch of turmeric for color—truly will make you feel like you're back in front of the Good Humor truck. If you're serving a crowd, make the sliceable, large-format version and drizzle on the syrup after slicing.

Two 14-ounce cans full-fat coconut milk (3½ cups)

1 cup (200 grams) sugar

⅓ cup (40 grams) cornstarch

½ teaspoon kosher salt, plus a pinch for the syrup

2 teaspoons (10 grams) pure vanilla extract or paste

Finely grated zest and juice of 1 medium orange (1 tablespoon zest, ½ cup juice)

Pinch of ground turmeric (optional)

1½ tablespoons (22 ml) freshly squeezed lemon juice

¼ cup (30 grams) toasted pistachios (salted is OK, too), coarsely chopped, for topping

1. In a medium saucepan off the heat, whisk together the coconut milk, ½ cup of the sugar, the cornstarch, and salt. Whisking constantly, cook the mixture over medium-high heat until it reaches a low boil and begins to thicken, 4 to 5 minutes. Reduce the heat to medium-low and continue to cook, whisking, until the mixture thickens and coats the back of a spoon, 2 to 3 more minutes. Remove from the heat, whisk in the vanilla and orange zest, and pour into a 9-inch glass or ceramic pie plate or six individual 6-ounce ramekins or small bowls.

2. Cool for 30 minutes (it's OK if a little skin forms), cover with plastic wrap, poke a few holes in the plastic with a toothpick, and chill until set, 2 to 2½ hours. While the malabi is chilling, in a small saucepan, bring the orange juice, remaining ½ cup sugar, and the pinch of turmeric (if using) and salt to a boil over high heat. Cook until the mixture forms large bubbles, is slightly foamy, and reduces to just under ½ cup, 4 to 5 minutes. Remove from the heat, stir in the lemon juice and orange zest, and cool completely. When the malabi is set, pour some of the syrup over the top and sprinkle with the pistachios. Serve with additional syrup.

Tangy Lime Blondies

MAKES 12 OR 16 BARS • ACTIVE TIME: 15 MINUTES
TOTAL TIME (INCLUDING COOLING TIME): 35 MINUTES

This one kicked around in my mind until I finally set out to make the perfect chewy, zingy, citrusy blondie based solely around the flavor of a lime. I was aiming for goes-with-coffee or after-school vibes, so I skipped a sweet icing and put all my recipe-conjuring powers into the blondie itself: slightly chewy (cakeyness is just around the corner if you overbake, so don't!), citrusy, tender, and pale. Yes, you'll end up with a bit of extra lime juice, but if you're anything like me, that'll get used up in a dressing, marinade, or glass of seltzer within hours. The crushed-up dried raspberries reinforce the zing and add a pop of color, since we all know we eat with our eyes.

- ⅔ cup (133 grams) granulated sugar
- 2 small limes
- 1½ sticks (6 ounces/ 189 grams) unsalted butter
- ⅓ cup (40 grams) confectioners' sugar
- 2 large eggs
- ½ teaspoon pure vanilla extract
- 1 cup (130 grams) all-purpose flour
- ½ teaspoon (2 grams) fine sea salt
- 5 dehydrated raspberries, crushed into powder

Preheat the oven to 325°F. Line an 8-inch square baking pan with parchment paper. Add the granulated sugar to a large mixing bowl. Finely zest one of the limes and half of the second lime (you'll zest the last half before serving). Rub the zest into the sugar with your fingers to release the citrus oils, 5 to 10 seconds. In a small microwave-safe bowl, microwave the butter in 10- or 15-second increments until the butter slumps but is still mostly opaque with a few melted spots, 25 to 30 seconds. Vigorously whisk in the butter and confectioners' sugar until smooth, 10 seconds. Whisk in the eggs and the vanilla until smooth, 10 to 20 seconds. Juice one of the limes (about 2 to 2½ tablespoons) directly into the batter and whisk vigorously again, 10 seconds (the mixture will appear slightly curdled). Gently fold in the flour and salt until just incorporated. Spread the batter evenly into the prepared pan; bake until the center is just set and pale and the edges are very lightly golden, 17 to 18 minutes. Cool completely, dust with the raspberry powder, zest the remaining lime half directly on top (save the juice for another use), and cut into 12 or 16 bars.

Priel Shabo of the late, great Bottarga restaurant (see page 90)

Elad Amitai, Chef/Owner of Hacarmel 40 (see page 112)

Michel Haviv, owner of Bazaar (see page 62)

Tikvah Yitzchak, juice queen of the Carmel Market (see page 28)

Fishmonger Rustum Mansour (see page 112), supplier to Hacarmel 40

Carmel Market Fruit purveyor Gershon Rabia (see page 39)

Mickey Perez, owner of Caffe Tamati (see page 228)

Chef Hila Alpert, whose Lali salad inspired one of my recipes (see page 192)

Acknowledgments

To Dan Perez and Nurit Kariv, my work family and creative inspirations. Dan, thanks for always bringing the light. Nurit, you make everything you touch more beautiful and delicious.

To my editor/goddess, Lucia Watson, thank you for your expertise, grace, and wisdom.

Lindsay Gordon, Farin Schlussel, Ashley Tucker, Maya Ono, Neda Dallal, Tracy Behar, Isabel McCarthy, and the entire Avery team: You are so good at what you do. Not to mention kind, thoughtful, and endlessly supportive through some very challenging times. I am more grateful than I can even express.

To Janis Donnaud, for making my deals, making me laugh, and making me better at what I do.

To Naama Malomet, how much we've done together in such a short time! Thank you for your talents, grace, and generosity through all the challenges. The best! Jazzie Morgan, you're beyond talented, beyond irreplaceable—all the beyonds. Galia Schipper, I love watching you grow as the world discovers what I knew from day one. Keep soaring.

To Leora Mietkewicz, for getting this started and for the flawless handover.

To Rosanne Kang, for your stylish eye and design advice on every book.

Vivian Saade, you are truly one of a kind. The best volunteer, friend, and foodie!

Karl Wagner, Marisa Robertson Textor, Melissa Roberts Matar, and Shelley Wiseman: Simply the best at what you do!

To the dedicated community of cooks who put these recipes through their paces, I'm eternally grateful for your watchful eyes and generosity of spirit. Thank you, Jackie Alpers, Stephanie Banyas, Danielle Centoni, Jodie Chase, Ruth Coleman, Danielle Colen, Danielle DeSiato Kuhn, Randy Eylmann, Julie Gruenbaum Fax, Nicole Fisher, Meghan Glass, Ingrid Goldfein, Lynn Harris, Meredith Kellman, Alyssa Langer, Michal Levine, Yael Offer, Wendy Paler, Fran Pine, Nicole Putzel, Rachel Ringler, Vivian Saade, Kirsten Schofield, Gayle Squires, Jessica Steinberg, Bonnie Stern, Tina Ujlaki, and Sharon Wieder.

To my family: The most loyal, loving bunch.

To Jay: Love you the most. My forever. XO

Index

D

E

F

M

N

O

P

Q

R

thai chili flakes
WHITE PEPPER
C.J.R. KESBEKE
AMSTERDAM
18.00
persian lime
OREGANO
SINGLE ORIGIN SPICES
BURLAP & BARREL
marash pepper
slow · small · simple
Bourbon Smoked Paprika
DILL
DUKKAH
URFA
green peppercorns
curry powder
slow · small · simple
Bourbon Smoked Pepper
CUMIN SEED
DRIED ROSEMARY
6.90
CAYENNE
RAS AL HANOUT
ground coriander
mustard
fennel
CHILI POWDER
CORIANDER SEED
whole peppercorns